⊙◙⅄□⋈

⊙∇I╥⊙⅄◇↑

ⵊ╥⊙ⅆ∇◇ʕ ⌘.

⋈○ⅆ⊙□⋈♁◇, ⌘◙.

Adinkra Alphabet

Charles M. Korankye, MD.

Adinkra Alphabet

The Adinkra Symbols as Alphabets & Their Hidden Meanings

Fourth Edition

Charles M. Korankye, MD.

First Edition, October 2015.

Second Edition, August 2016

Third Edition, July 2017

ISBN: 978-1-947478-06-0

Library of Congress Control Number: 2021908686

Registration Number: TX 8-164-376 (Adinkra Alphabet)

Registration Number: TXu 1-971-068 (Adinkra Tree of Life)

Please address all inquiries to:

Charles Korankye,

www.adinkraalphabet.com

Cover illustration by Charles Korankye

Cover design by Baffour Annor

Printed in the United States of America,

May 2021.

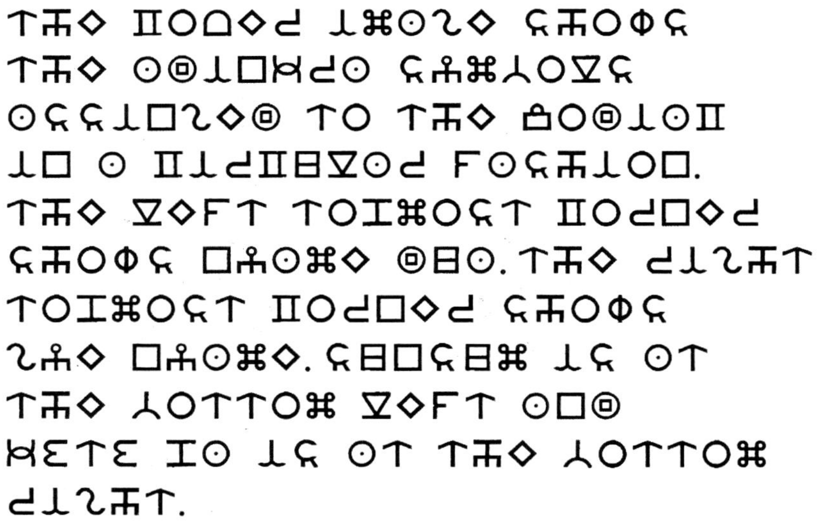

Cover Illustration

The cover image shows the Adinkra symbols assigned to the zodiac in a circular fashion. The left topmost corner shows Nyame Dua. The right topmost corner shows Gye Nyame. Sunsum is at the bottom left and Kɛtɛ Pa is at the bottom right.

This book is dedicated with love to my wife Nana Ama and our children Kweku, Esi and Kwesi for the beautiful Light they transmit to me every day and to all Adinkra Alphabet lovers and followers all over the world.

Preface

I am very excited about what Adinkra Alphabet has become. It has come to represent Ghanaian heritage and this heritage extend to the whole of Africa.

The main purpose of Adinkra Alphabet is to be able to write all the languages in Ghana in our own native characters. Writing in this manner gives us a sense of ethnic identity as the characters that form a word now has a more deeper meaning to us than using English, Latin or Greek characters. The caution that I have for lovers of Adinkra alphabet is to learn to write with Adinkra Alphabet through the spirit and soul of the Adinkra symbols. Learning Adinkra alphabet without knowing the Adinkra symbol associated with the alphabet will be meaningless.

Writing this way is not something new. Ethiopians, Chinese, Korean and Japanese all write with native characters.

In this book, the complete Adinkra Alphabet characters of the four major Ghanaian languages; Akan, Ewe, Ga(Dangbe) and Dagbani are demonstrated. This removes diacritics, double articulation, and accents, making it easy to write the respective languages with Adinkra Alphabet.

My first book Adinkra Alphabet has 26 characters just as in English alphabet. The second Edition of Adinkra Alphabet has 28 characters with the introduction of ɛ and ɔ. This book contains 54 characters which is almost double of the second edition characters. To make the study of this book easy I have developed the Adinkra card game. The card game contains all the 52 major Adinkra Alphabet characters in this book and demonstrate their virtues, numerical value, elemental properties, and astronomical values. I highly recommend the study of this book with the Adinkra card game for a full exploration of Adinkra alphabet and to make the understanding easier. To further make writing with the characters easy I have developed simplified Adinkra alphabet characters that are much simpler to hand-write with. I again caution that these characters are used bearing in mind the Adinkra symbol from which the character is derived.

Learning the Adinkra Tree of Life (ATOL) will help one understand the hidden meanings of the Adinkra symbols and also the Adinkra numbering system. The Adinkra Flower of Life (AFOL) link all the meanings, numbers and characters used in this book.

I thank all Adinkra Alphabet lovers and followers for your support and for making Adinkra Alphabet into what it has become.

Foreword

It is with great pleasure that I write to introduce the Adinkra Alphabet book. Indeed, Dr. Korankye has done a tremendous job writing about the Adinkra symbols and has also shown how it could be used as alphabets. He starts by explaining the hidden meanings behind the symbols so that as you use them you become more familiar with their meanings.

Dr. Korankye has bequeathed to Ghana and the rest of Africa indigenous characters for writing. As mentioned elsewhere in the book, the Chinese, Japanese, Koreans, Indians etc. have their unique characters for writing and I am happy that Dr. Korankye has been able to develop the Adinkra characters that will pave the way for Ghana and the rest of Africa to use these unique characters for writing.

Prior to reading the book, I had always thought that the Adinkra symbols were used as designs in clothes. Lifting the characters to the level where they can be used as a form of writing makes the characters assume a more important role in educating our children.

The hope is that the Ministry of Education in Ghana will take a critical look at the work by Dr. Korankye with the view of adopting it in Ghanaian schools so that a parallel form of writing using the Adinkra characters could be taught in our schools. In this way, Ghana, in some years to come, can also be proud of having its own form of writing.

The book is a must read by all Ghanaians and indeed all Africans for that matter.

Peter Annor, PhD.

Acknowledgements

I wish to express my sincerest thanks to Peter Annor, PhD whose guidance and support inspired the creation of this book.

I am also very thankful to Prof. Elizabeth Amoah, University of Ghana, for taking time to review my work.

I wish to thank Baffour Annor who taught me the basics of Adobe Photoshop and helped me in the creation of the symbols used in this book.

I would like to acknowledge Marvin Boateng for writing to me personally about adding Akan characters ɛ and ɔ and taking time to write with Adinkra Alphabet. Thank you for your passion and interest using Adinkra Alphabet.

I also would like to thank Stella Kafui Tetteh for taking time to write with Adinkra Alphabet and sharing her many writings with me on Facebook. My thanks also go to Stella for reviewing the Ghana national anthem in Ewe and ensuring that the correct Ewe alphabet characters are used.

The use of Kasahorow keyboard made it easy to correctly type out the Akan characters and I am thankful to the guys who created it.

I am also thankful to Man Amarteyfio for reviewing the Ghana national anthem in Ga to make sure that the correct Ga alphabet characters are used.

I am also thankful to Bertha Gorman who wrote to me about the deeper meaning of Adinkra symbol Fihankra.

I wish to thank Alhassan Mohammed Amidu and Issa Mariatu Quibtiyya for taking time to write the Ghana national Anthem in Dagbani. I am also thankful to Alhassan Lukman for sending me an audio file of the Ghana national anthem in Dagbani. Many thanks also go to Gifty Yeboah for working with Mohammed Amidu, Issa Mariatu Quibtiyya and Alhassan Lukman in the preparation of the Dagbani Alphabet.

I am also thankful to Nana Adjoa Adobea Asante, Director of Ghana National Folklore board for her insight on the proper virtue for Ɛse Ne Tɛkrɛma.

Contents

Preface......ix
Foreword......xi
Acknowledgements......xiii
Introduction......1
History of Adinkra Symbols......3
Adinkra Alphabet......5
Symbol - Letter Assignment......7
Table of Vowels......12
Akan Table of Consonants......14
Meaning of Symbols......26
Meaning of Characters – Vowels......27
1. **Adinkrahene**......27
2. **Ɛban**......28
3. **Ɛse Ne Tɛkrɛma**......29
4. **Nyame Biribi Wɔ Soro**......30
5. **Nea Onnim No Sua A, Ohu**......31
Meaning of Characters - Consonants......32
6. **Bi Nka Bi**......32
7. **Ɔwo Foro Adobɛ**......33
8. **Dame-Dame**......34
9. **Fawohodie**......35
10. **Gye Nyame**......36

11. **Hwemudua** 37
12. **Ɛpa** 38
13. **Kintinkantan** 39
14. **Mmerɛ Dane** 40
15. **Mpatapɔ** 41
16. **Nkyimu** 42
17. **Pempamsie** 43
18. **Denkyɛm** 44
19. **Asase Ye Duru** 45
20. **Sankɔfa** 46
21. **Aya** 47
22. **Bese Saka** 48
23. **Wawa Aba** 49
24. **Akokɔnan** 50
25. **Duafe** 51
26. **Fihankra** 52
27. **Dwennimmɛn** 53
28. **Ɔsram Ne Nsoromma** 54
29. **Funtunfunefu Dɛnkyɛmfunefu** 55
30. **Mpuanum** 56
31. **Hye Wonhye** 57
32. **Mate Masie** 58
33. **Ɔkɔdeɛ Mmɔwerɛ** 59

34. Nyansapɔ ... 60
35. Nsaa ... 61
36. Akoma ... 62
37. Nyame Nwu Na Mawu. ... 63
Special Characters – Ga ... 64
38. Nkɔnsɔnkɔnsɔn ... 64
Special Characters – Dagbani. ... 65
39. Mframadan ... 65
40. Kɛtɛ Pa ... 66
41. Nkyinkyim ... 67
Special Characters – Astronomy ... 68
42. Nsoromma ... 68
43. Ɔsram ... 69
44. Boa Me Na Me Mmoa Wo ... 70
45. Ɔdɔ Nyera Fie Kwan ... 71
46. Fofo ... 72
47. 1 Akoben ... 73
47.2 Akofena ... 74
48. 1 Gyawu Atikɔ ... 75
48.2 Kwatakye Atikɔ ... 76
49. Musuyideɛ ... 77
50. Owuo Atwedeɛ ... 78
51. Sunsum ... 79

52. Nyame Dua 80
Adinkra Tree of Life 90
Adinkra Flower of Life 97
Adinkra Virtues 101
Adinkra Numerology 105
Explanation of Numerology 109
Geometrical Explanation of Numerology 110
Adinkra Alphabet Elemental properties 112
Rules for Assigning Elemental Properties 115
Triplicity Rulership 116
Table of Colors and their Symbology 117
Adinkra Colors and their Meaning 118
Adinkra Zodiac 119
Adinkra Astronomy 120
Adinkra Astronomical Sign and Day of the week Governed 121
Adinkra Astronomical Sign and Given Akan Names 122
Application of Adinkra Alphabet and Numbers 123
Ghana Patriotic Song-Akan 124
Ghana National Anthem-English 130
Patriotic Song, Akan 136
Yen Ara Asase Ni 137
Ghana National Anthem English 139

Patriotic Song, Ewe 141

Patriotic Song, Ga 143

Patriotic Song, Dagbani 145

African Countries 147

Numbering System 155

Original Adinkra Symbols 159

1. **Adinkrahene (a, ⊙, 3)** 159
2. **Bi Nka Bi (b, ⅄, 40)** 159
3. **Ɔwo Foro Adobɛ (c, Π, 6)** 159
4. **Dame-Dame (d, ◎, 4)** 160
5. **Ɛban (e, ◇, 20)** 160
6. **Fawohodie (f, Ϝ, 9)** 160
7. **Gye Nyame (g, ᘔ, 0)** 161
8. **Hwemudua (h, ╦, 50)** 161
9. **Ɛse Ne Tɛkrɛma (I, ⊥, 30)** 161
10. **Ɛpa (j, ✘, 60)** 162
11. **Kintinkantan (k, ⋈, 70)** 162
12. **Mmerɛ Dane (l, ⧖, 80)** 162
13. **Mpatapɔ (m, ⌘, 90)** 163
14. **Nkyimu (n, ☐, 100)** 163
15. **Nyame Biribi Wɔ Soro (o, O, 5)** 163
16. **Pempamsie (p, ⌶, 2)** 164
17. **Denkyɛm (q, Ψ, 8)** 164

18. **Asase Ye Duru (r, ᑯ, 200)** 164
19. **Sankɔfa (s, ʕ, 1)** 165
20. **Aya (t, ᛏ, 300)** 165
21. **Nea Onnim No Sua A, Ohu (u, ⊟, 7)** 165
22. **Bese Saka (v, ⌂, 400)** 166
23. **Wawa Aba (w, Φ, 500)** 166
24. **Akokɔnan (x, Ⱨ, 600)** 166
25. **Duafe (y, ♁, 700)** 167
26. **Fihankra (z, ⏍, 800)** 167
27. **Dwennimmɛn (ɛ, Ɛ, 10)** 167
28. **Ɔsram Ne Nsoromma (ɔ, Ↄ, 900)** 168
29. **Hye Wonhye (ƒ, ϒ, 1000)** 168
30. **Nyame Nnwu Na Mawu (ts, ✕, 2000)** 168
31. **Nyansapɔ (kp, Φ, 3000)** 169
32. **Nsaa (ny, ⊞, 4000)** 169
33. **Mpuanum (dz, ⵅ, 5000)** 169
34. **Akoma (ʋ, ᑫ, 6000)** 170
35. **Funtunfunefu-Dɛnkyɛmfunefu** 170
36. **Nkɔnsɔnkɔnsɔn (ŋ, ⵣ, 8000)** 170
37. **Ɔkɔdeɛ Mmɔwerɛ (ɣ, ǂ, 9000)** 171
38. **Mframadan (ch, ⊠, 10,000)** 171
39. **Mate Masie (gb, ⵙ, 11,000)** 171

40. **Nkyinkyim (ʒ, ꟻ, 12,000)** 172
41. **Kɛtɛ Pa (sh, ⋕ , 13,000)** 172
42. **Nsoromma (☉, ⊥, 14,000)** 172
43. **Ɔsram (☾, ∪ , 15,000)** 173
44. **Boa Me Na Me Mmoa Wo** 173
(☿, ⧊ , 16,000) 173
45. **Ɔdɔ Nyera Fie Kwan** 173
(♀ , ⫝̸ , 17,000) 173
46. **Fofo (⊕,)(, 18,000)** 174
47. **1Akobɛn (♂ , ⫫ , 19,000)** 174
47.2Akofena (♂ , ⫫ , 19,000) 174
48. **1 Kwatakye Atikɔ (♃, ෧ , 20,000)** 175
48.2 **Gyawu Atikɔ (♃ , ෧ , 20,000)** 175
49. **Musuyideɛ (♄, ▽ , 21,000)** 175
50. **Owuo Atwedeɛ (♅, ⊓ , 22,000)** 176

51. **Sunsum (♆, ◬, 23,000)** 176

52. **Nyame Dua (☥, ϒ, 24,000)** 176

Proverbs, Sayings and Objects associated with Adinkra symbols 177

Phonetics 185

Correspondence between Airflow in sound, The Adinkra Tree of Life and the Kabbalistic Tree of Life 188

Adinkra Vowels and their Sound 190

Adinkra Consonants and their Sound 191

Akan Table of Vowels 194

Akan Table of Consonants 195

Ewe Table of Vowels 198

Ewe Table of Consonants 199

Ga (Dangbe) Table of Vowels 202

Ga (Dangbe) Table of Consonants 203

Dagbani Table of Vowels 206

Dagbani Table of Consonants 207

Adinkra Alphabet Phonetic Vowels Diagram 212

Tongue Position of Vowels 213

International Phonetic Alphabet (IPA) Vowels chart 214

Adinkra Alphabet Phonetic, Consonants Chart-Lips, Teeth and Tongue 215

Adinkra Alphabet Phonetic, Consonants Chart-Palate and Throat 216

Airway Position of Consonants 217

Akan Pronunciation-Vowels 218

Akan Pronunciation - Consonants 221

Akan Diacritics 225

Akan Co-articulated 225

Adinkra Alphabet Akan Phonetic Vowel Position Table 226

Adinkra Alphabet Akan Phonetic, Consonants Chart-Lips, Teeth and Tongue 227

Adinkra Alphabet Akan Phonetic, Consonants Chart-Palate and Throat 228

Ewe Pronunciation-Vowels 229

Ewe Pronunciation - Consonants 231

Adinkra Alphabet Ewe Phonetic Vowel Position Table 234

Adinkra Alphabet Ewe Phonetic, Consonants Chart-Lips, Teeth and Tongue 235

Adinkra Alphabet Ewe Phonetic, Consonants Chart-Palate and Throat 236

Ga Pronunciation-Vowels 237

Ga Pronunciation - Consonants 239

Adinkra Alphabet Ga Phonetic Vowel Position Table .. 242

Adinkra Alphabet Ga Phonetic- Consonants Chart-Lips, Teeth and Tongue 243

Introduction

Adinkra symbols have existed for many years in Ghana and other parts of West Africa. In Ghana, they are a means of communication by the Akan people. The symbols have always intrigued me and have had such profound effect on me since I started studying the hidden meanings behind them. It is difficult for the average person to decipher the hidden meanings behind the symbols. By assigning letters to the symbols it impacts a deeper meaning to words and also bring the hidden meanings of the symbols for everyday use.

I have endeavored to make the symbols into an alphabet system and have also assigned each of the symbols a vowel or consonant. The symbols are already familiar to the people of Ghana and other regions in West Africa and therefore studying the alphabet system created with the symbols will be natural and easy for them. My hope is that the use of the Adinkra alphabet will deepen the understanding of the deeper meanings behind the symbols and help create a unified language system for the Akans, the people of Ghana and possibly West Africa as a whole.

Each symbol has three levels of meaning: the literal meaning, the physical meaning and the metaphysical meaning. The literal meaning is the direct meaning of the symbol as it is pronounced. The physical meaning is the extension of the literal meaning to society. Metaphysical meaning is the extension of the literal and physical meaning to the Divine.

In using these symbols as alphabets, I have had to trim the shapes of the original symbols and also modify the shapes of some of the symbols to make it easy to use in writing. Forty-two symbols were used in the Adinkra alphabet system and fifty-two symbols were used in the Adinkra numbering system.

History of Adinkra Symbols

Adinkra are visual symbols, originally created by the Akan that represent concepts or aphorisms. Traditionally the symbols were printed on cotton fabrics with wooden comb-like tool and stamps made from calabash with Adinkra patterns cut on them. In addition to being printed on fabrics, Adinkra are also used in pottery, architecture, logos and advertising. Adinkra cloths were traditionally only worn by royalty and spiritual leaders for funeral and other very special occasions. However, they are now worn by anyone for various occasions.

The Adinkra symbols have existed in ancient times and the exact date for the origin of the symbols are unknown. There are many different accounts to the origin of the symbols.

One account dates the symbols to the end of the 1818 Asante–Gyaman war. The then Asantehene Nana Osei Bonsu Panyin defeated the king of Gyaman, Nana Kofi Adinkra in the Ivory Coast. The defeated soldiers of Nana Kofi Adinkra are said to include craftsmen who introduced the art of making cloths with Adinkra patterns stamped in them. There are indications from history however that Adinkra symbols existed before this date.

Adinkra also means "farewell" or "good-bye" in the Akan language. It is said that the cloth with its symbols derived its name from being used to say farewell or good-bye to departed souls during funerals.

The use of Adinkra in communication and as a writing system has existed for many years among the Akan people of Ghana. In communication messages are transmitted either through the use of individual symbols or by use of a combination of symbols. Mpatapo

(⌘) as a symbol means reconciliation between two factions. Mpatapɔ, Gye Nyame and Bi Nka Bi

(⌘ᘔ⅄) together in that order will mean we agree to reconcile today under heaven, and we will exist as brothers/sisters and will not bite one another. Ɛpa and Bi Nka Bi (᙭⅄) in that order means equality and justice before the law for all.

Communication using different symbols can be created by combining multiple symbols such as the combination of Adinkrahene and Gye Nyame to form Nyame Yɛ Ohene. There is also the combination of Osram and Nsoromma to form Osram ne Nsoromma.

Adinkra Alphabet

I created the Adinkra alphabet system to bridge the gap in communication between the ancient and traditional Akan system of communication using symbols and the current mode of language communication in Ghana.

For example, a word such as LOVE (⊻O⌂◇) will carry the meaning of love and also the virtues, the moral and metaphysical significance of all the symbols in the word. In the word Love (⊻O⌂◇) for example, each symbolic Adinkra letter carries three levels of meaning; the Literal meaning, Physical meaning and Metaphysical meaning. Hence the word "Love" spelled using the Adinkra alphabet system conveys a greater depth in meaning and application. Love in English carries the virtues of Constancy (L), Beauty (O), Resourcefulness (V) and Charity (E). In Akan Ɔdɔ (⊃⊚⊃) means love and carries the virtues of Harmony (Ɔ) and Judgement (D). In Ewe Lɔlɔ (⊻⊃⊻⊃) means love and carries the virtues of Constancy (L) and Harmony (Ɔ). In Ga Sumɔ (ዩ⊟⌘⊃) means love and carries the virtues of Wisdom (S), Service (U), Reconciliation (M) and Harmony (Ɔ). In Dagbani Yuri (ቶ⊟ᑯ⊥) means love and carries the virtues of Cleanliness (Y), Service (U), Providence (R) and Growth (I).

Each letter of the Adinkra alphabet is derived from a unique Adinkra symbol. The primary Adinkra alphabet system consist of 7 vowels and 21 consonants making a total of 28 letters.

The extended Adinkra alphabet consist of 7 vowels and 35 consonants to make a total of 42 letters. The extended Adinkra alphabet has characters for the four major Ghanaian languages, Akan, Ewe, Ga and Dagbani. Nyame Dua act as a number marker and for apostrophe in Dagbani.

The primary Adinkra alphabet system is modeled along the English alphabet system as English is the primary language of instruction in Ghana. Two additional symbols have been added to the primary Adinkra alphabet system; which are Dwennimmɛn and Ɔsram Ne Nsoromma for characters Ɛ and Ɔ respectively to make a total of 28 characters.

There are over 100 Adinkra symbols however, in the creation of the alphabet system I used some of the common and most familiar symbols.

Adinkra Alphabet characters are simplified versions of the Adinkra symbol from which the alphabet is derived. I further simplified the characters in the creation of the Simplified Adinkra Alphabet for ease of writing.

Symbol - Letter Assignment

The Symbol – Letter assignments were based on the sound of the first letter of the symbol, the prominent vowel or consonant sound, shape of symbol or its meaning. Each of the special characters for the Ghanaian languages Akan, Ewe, Ga and Dagbani is derived from a specific Adinkra symbol.

Vowels:

Alphabet **a** and ɔ have the same first letter as the symbol they represent; **a** for Adinkrahene () and **ɔ** for Ɔsram Ne Nsoromma (). Ɛban () was assigned to letter **e** as the first letter Ɛ is close to e. In the remaining four vowels where the first letters are different, the prominent vowel sound in the phrase was used. The remaining four vowels, Nea Onnim No Sua A, Ohu, Nyame Biri Wɔ Soro, Dwennimmɛn and Ɛse Ne Tekrɛma were assigned as follows: Nea Onnim No Sua A, Ohu () for **u** due to the **u** in 'Sua' and 'Ohu' which sound prominently in them. Nyame Biribi Wɔ Soro () for **o** due to the **o** in the last word Soro which sounds prominently in it. Dwennimmɛn () for **ɛ** due to ɛ at the end of the word which sounds prominently in it and Ɛse Ne Tekrɛma () was assigned to **I** as the prominent **e** sound in it is close to **i** sound.

Consonants:

Adinkra alphabet **b, d, f, g, h, k, m, n p, s, w,** were selected as their first letter are the same as the symbol they represent.

The letter **c** was assigned to Ɔwo Foro Adobɛ ( ) as the first letter Ɔ resembles the letter **c**.

The letter **x** was assigned to Akokɔnan ( ) due to the cross in the symbol. Ɛpa ( ) literally means handcuff which has something to do with the judiciary system that is why the letter **j** was assigned to Ɛpa (The Ɛpa symbol predate slavery).

Aya ( ) appears as **t** turned upside down and that is why the letter **t** was assigned to it. Duafe ( ) appears as **y** turned upside down and that is why the letter **y** was assigned to it. The modified symbol of Bese Saka appears as **v** turned upside down so Bese Saka ( ) was assigned the letter **v**.

The remaining symbols are Mmerɛ Dane, Denkyɛm, Asase Ye Duru and Fihankra. Mmerɛ Dane ( ) was assigned to the letter **l** due to the proximity of **m** to **l**. Asase Ye Duru ( ) was assigned to **r** due to the letter r in Duru which sounds prominently in it. Denkyɛm ( ) symbol resembles q the most so it was assigned the letter **q**. Fihankra ( ) literally means house or compound. This was the last consonant to be assigned so it was paired with the last English alphabet **z**.

Special Characters: I considered the shape of the characters a lot in assigning special characters.

Akan: Akan vowel characters ɛ and ɔ were assigned as mentioned above.

Ɛwɛ: Akoma () resembles ʋ the most so it was assigned to it. Ɔkɔdeɛ Mmɔwerɛ ( ) resembles ɣ the most so it was assigned to it. Funtunfunefu Dɛnkyɛmfunefu has letter d as the first letter in Dɛnkyɛmfunefu so it was assigned to ɖ. The first character of Nsaa () is N so it was assigned to ny. The p in Nyansapɔ ( ) sounds prominently in it so it was assigned to kp. Mate Masie, Mpuanum, Hye Wonhye and Nyame Nwu Na Mawu were randomly assigned to gb, dz, ƒ and ts respectively.

Dagbani: ŋ is close to n so it was assigned to Nkɔnsɔnkɔnsɔn (). Nkyinkyim () symbol resemble ʒ so it was assigned to it. Sh is the last two words in hash and Kɛtɛ Pa () is close to the hash sign so it was assigned to it. Mframadan ()was randomly assigned to ch.

Ga: ŋ is assigned to Nkɔnsɔnkɔnsɔn as explained above.

Zodiac Characters:

The character of Hye Wonhye () resembles the ram character so it was assigned to Aries. Taurus the bull was assigned to Nyame Nwu Na Mawu (). Nyansapɔ () has two lines going through it so it was assigned to the twin zodiac, Gemini. Nsaa () has 4 windows in it so it was assigned to the 4th zodiac, Cancer. Mpuanum () means "5 tufts of hair" and it was assigned to the 5th zodiac, Leo. The heart symbol, Akoma () was assigned to the virgin zodiac, Virgo. Libra zodiac represent scales or balance and it was assigned to Funtunfunefu Dɛnkyɛmfunefu (), the symbol of democracy and unity. The sharp arrows of Nkɔnsɔnkɔnsɔn () resembles a scorpion so it was assigned to it. The symbol of Ɔkɔdeɛ Mmɔwerɛ () resembles bow and arrow so it was assigned to Sagittarius. Capricorn's have the characteristics of being able to thrive in hostile environment, so it was assigned to Mframadan (), "wind resistant house". Aquarius is the age of knowledge and understanding so it was assigned to Mate Masie (), symbol of understanding. Nkyinkyim () is freedom of twisting and adaptation so it was assigned to Pisces, fish which lives in the vast twisting and turning ocean.

Astronomical signs:

Nsoromma ( ) means sun so it was assigned to it. Ɔsram ( ) means moon so it was assigned to it. Tuesday has Mars energy, so it was assigned to Akoben ( ) or Akofena ( ). Thursday has Thor energy, so it was assigned to Kwatakye ( ) and Gyawu Atikɔ ( ). Boa Me Na Me Mmoa Wo ( ) shows symmetry between masculine and feminine energy, so it was assigned to Wednesday, which falls on the middle of the week. Venus is for love and beauty, so it was assigned to Ɔdɔ Nyera Fie Kwan ( ). Saturn is for Saturday, a day of rest and reflection so it was assigned to Musuyideɛ ( ). Fofo ( ) is a symbol of mortality, so it was assigned to Earth. Uranus is a governor of the sky, so it was assigned to Sunsum ( ), “Soul”.

Table of Vowels

Alphabet	Adinkra Alphabet	Adinkra Name	English Translation
A/a		Adinkrahene	Chief of all the Adinkra symbols
E/e		Ɛban	Fence
I/i		Ɛse Ne Tɛkrɛma	The Teeth and the Tongue

Alphabet	Adinkra Alphabet	Adinkra Name	English Translation
O/o		Nyame Biribi Wɔ Soro	God's something is in the heavens.
U/u		Nea Onnim No Sua A, Ohu	He/She who does not know, can know from learning.
Ɛ/ɛ		Dwennimmɛn	Ram's horns
Ɔ/ɔ		Ɔsram Ne Nsoromma	The Moon and the Star

Akan Table of Consonants

Alphabet	Adinkra Alphabet	Adinkra Name	English Translation
B/b		Bi Nka Bi	Bite not one Another
C/c		Ɔwɔ Foro Adobɛ	A snake climbs the raffia palm
D/d		Dame-Dame	Board game

Adinkra Alphabet

Alphabet	Adinkra Alphabet	Adinkra Name	English Translation
F/f		Fawohodie	Freedom
G/g		Gye Nyame	Except God
H/h	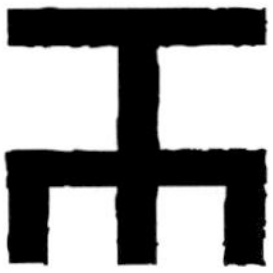	Hwemudua	Measuring Stick

Adinkra Alphabet

Alphabet	Adinkra Alphabet	Adinkra Name	English Translation
J/j		Ɛpa	Handcuffs
K/k		Kintinkantan	Puffed up extravagance
L/l		Mmerɛ Dane	Time changes

Adinkra Alphabet

Alphabet	Adinkra Alphabet	Adinkra Name	English Translation
M/m	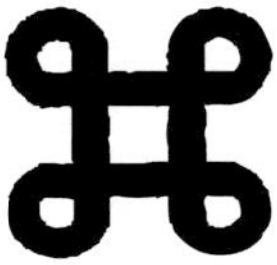	Mpatapɔ	Knot of reconciliation
N/n	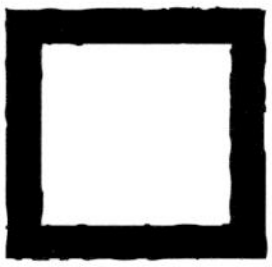	Nkyimu	Crossed divisions made on adinkra cloth before stamping
P/p		Pempamsie	Sew to preserve

Alphabet	Adinkra Alphabet	Adinkra Name	English Translation
Q/q	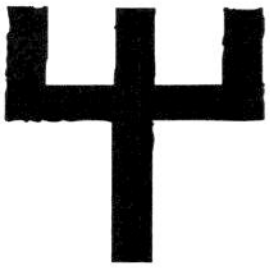	Denkyɛm	Crocodile
R/r		Asase Ye Duru	The Earth has weight (Gravity)
S/s	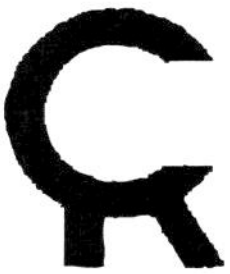	Sankɔfa	Go back and take

Adinkra Alphabet

Alphabet	Adinkra Alphabet	Adinkra Name	English Translation
T/t	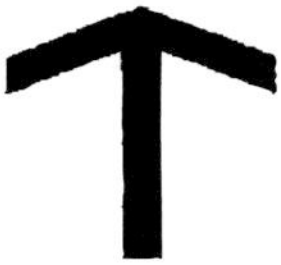	Aya	Fern
V/v		Bese Saka	Sack of cola nuts
W/w		Wawa Aba	Seed of the wawa tree

Adinkra Alphabet

Alphabet	Adinkra Alphabet	Adinkra Name	English Translation
X/x	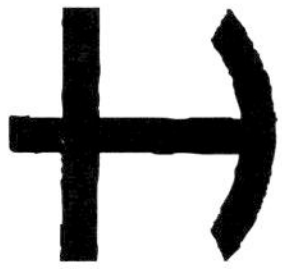	Akokɔnan	The legs of a hen
Y/y	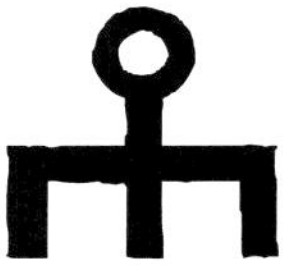	Duafe	Wooden comb
Z/z		Fihankra	You did not say goodbye when you left

Adinkra Alphabet

Alphabet	Adinkra Alphabet	Adinkra Name	English Translation
CH/ch		Mframadan	Wind resistant house
Đ/ɖ		Funtunfunefu Dɛnkyɛmfunefu	Conjoined crocodile
DZ/dz	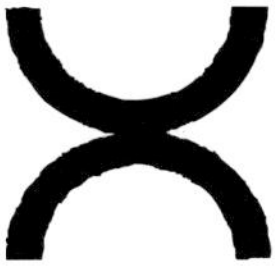	Mpuanum	Tusk of five

Adinkra Alphabet

Alphabet	Adinkra Alphabet	Adinkra Name	English Translation
X/x		Hye Wonhye	That which cannot be burnt
GB/gb		Mate Masie	What I hear, I keep
Ɣ/ɣ		Ɔkɔdeɛ Mmɔwerɛ	Talons of an Eagle

Alphabet	Adinkra Alphabet	Adinkra Name	English Translation
KP/kp		Nyansapɔ	Wisdom knot
NY/ny		Nsaa	Hand woven fabric
Ŋ/ ŋ		Nkɔnsɔnkɔnsɔn	Linked chains

Adinkra Alphabet

Alphabet	Adinkra Alphabet	Adinkra Name	English Translation
SH/sh		Kɛtɛ Pa	Good bed
TS/ts		Nyame Nwu Na Mawu	God never die; therefore, I do not die
Ʊ/ʊ		Akoma	Heart

Adinkra Alphabet

Alphabet	Adinkra Alphabet	Adinkra Name	English Translation
X/x		Nkyinkyim	Twisting's
☥		Nyame Dua	Tree of God

Meaning of Symbols

The Adinkra symbols have three levels of meaning consisting of the literal meaning, the physical meaning and the metaphysical meaning. The literal meaning is derived from the name of the symbol as it is pronounced. The physical meaning is the extension of the literal meaning to society. Metaphysical meaning is the extension of the literal and physical meaning to the Cosmic or Divine.

Each symbol used in the alphabet system is assigned a unique alphabet. All the symbols used are assigned a numerical value. Numbers zero to nine were assigned based on their position on the Adinkra Tree of Life and this impact special meaning to those numbers. The meaning of the numbers is explained in the geometrical explanation of numerology (pages 110 and 111). Nyame Dua is used as a number marker whenever necessary.

Meaning of Characters – Vowels

1. Adinkrahene

Original Adinkra Symbol:

Adinkra Alphabet – A/a

Numerical value – 3

Literal meaning: Adinkra, hene (Chief or King).

"Chief of all the adinkra symbols". All the other symbols are said to have been designed from this symbol.

Physical meaning – To act in a leadership role and inspire others.

Metaphysical meaning – It symbolizes greatness, charisma, and leadership.

2. Ɛban

Original Adinkra symbol:

Adinkra Alphabet – E/e

Numerical value – 20

Literal meaning: Ɛban (fence).

“fence”.

Physical meaning - A home with a fence around it is considered an ideal residence.

Metaphysical meaning – Symbolizes love, safety, and security.

3. Ɛse Ne Tɛkrɛma

Original Adinkra Symbol:

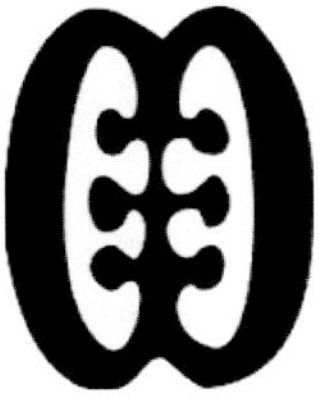

Adinkra Alphabet – I/i

Numerical value – 30

Literal meaning: Ɛse (Teeth), Tɛkrɛma (Tongue).

"the teeth and the tongue".

Physical meaning - The teeth and the tongue play interdependent roles in the mouth. They need to work together although they may come in conflict.

Metaphysical meaning – Friendship, unity, and interdependence.

4. Nyame Biribi Wɔ Soro

Original Adinkra Symbol:

Adinkra Alphabet – O/o

Numerical value – 5

Literal meaning: Nyame (God), Biribi (Something), Soro (heaven).

"God's something is in the heavens".

Physical meaning – God dwells in the heavens and he answers prayers.

Metaphysical meaning – Seek God in all your endeavors. Always strife to better yourself.

5. Nea Onnim No Sua A, Ohu

Original Adinkra Symbol:

Adinkra Alphabet - U/u

Numerical value – 7

Literal meaning: Nea (He/She), Onnim No (Does not know), Sua (Study), Ohu (Knows).

"He/She who does not know, will know from learning".

Symbol of geometry and the perfect symmetry in nature.

Physical meaning – Practice makes one perfect.

Metaphysical meaning – Symbolizes perseverance, service, and hard work in the acquisition of knowledge.

Meaning of Characters - Consonants

6. Bi Nka Bi

Original Adinkra Symbol:

Adinkra Alphabet – B/b

Numerical value – 40

Literal meaning: Bi (one), Nka (Bite not).

"Bite not one another".

Physical meaning – This symbol caution against negative actions towards one another such as cheating, stealing, anger etc.

Metaphysical meaning – Symbolizes peace, harmony, and brotherliness.

7. Ɔwo Foro Adobɛ

Original Adinkra Symbol:

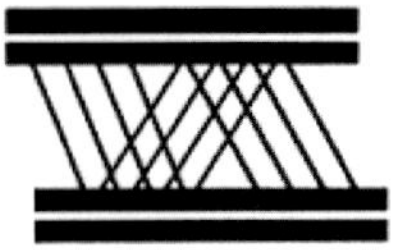

Adinkra Alphabet – C/c

Numerical value – 6

Literal meaning: Ɔwo (Snake), Foro (Climb), Adobɛ (Raffia palm).

"A snake climbs the raffia palm". It is normally difficult for snakes to climb thorny trees and therefore when it does, it has accomplished a herculean task.

Physical meaning – Signifies persistence and diligence to achieve success.

Metaphysical meaning – Symbolizes steadfastness and prudence.

8. Dame-Dame

Original Adinkra Symbol:

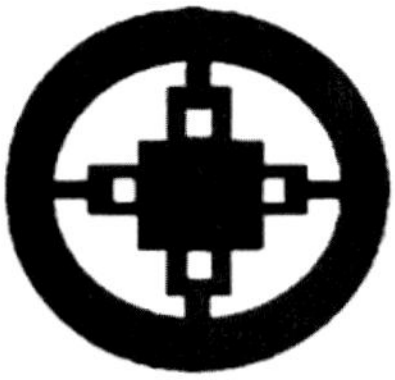

Adinkra Alphabet – D/d

Numerical value – 4

Literal meaning: Name of a board game.

"Ghana's draught (10X10 checkerboard game)".

Physical meaning – Symbolizes Intelligence and ingenuity.

Metaphysical meaning – The correct application of judgment and prudence to life.

9. Fawohodie

Original Adinkra Symbol:

Adinkra Alphabet – F/f

Numerical value – 9.

Literal meaning: Fawohodie (Freedom).

"Independence".

Physical meaning – Independence comes with its responsibility.

Metaphysical meaning – We create our own destiny. We must work for the things that we wish for in life.

10.Gye Nyame

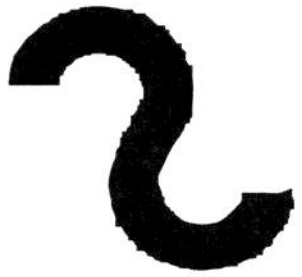

Original Adinkra Symbol:

Adinkra Alphabet – G/g

Numerical value: Zero.

Literal meaning: Gye (Except), Nyame (God).

“Except God”.

Physical meaning – Out of nothingness (space) came the universe. God is beyond the physical universe.

Metaphysical meaning – Symbolizes the omnipotent, omniscience and omnipresent power of God.

11.Hwemudua

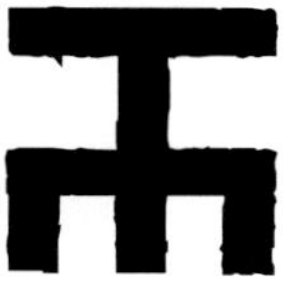

Original Adinkra Alphabet:

Adinkra Alphabet – H/h

Numerical value – 50

Literal meaning: Hwemu (Measure) Dua (Stick)

"measuring stick".

Physical meaning – Symbol stresses the need to strive for the best quality in all endeavors whether in production of goods or in human services.

Metaphysical meaning – Symbolizes strive towards perfection.

12.Ɛpa

Original Adinkra Symbol:

Adinkra Alphabet – J/j

Numerical value – 60

Literal meaning: Ɛpa (Handcuffs).

"Handcuffs".

This symbol predate slavery.

Physical meaning – A symbol of the uncompromising nature of the law to offenders and discourages slavery.

Metaphysical meaning – We should have boundaries for our daily life and avoid extremes.

13.Kintinkantan

Original Adinkra Symbol:

Adinkra Alphabet – K/k

Numerical value – 70

Literal meaning: Kintin (Puffed up), Kantan (Extravagance).

"Puffed up extravagance".

Physical meaning – Symbolize the nature of some individuals who are arrogant, pompous and bossy.

Metaphysical meaning – Humility and all life must be valued.

14.Mmerɛ Dane

Original Adinkra Symbol:

Adinkra Alphabet – L/l

Numerical value – 80

Literal meaning: Mmerɛ (Time), Dane (Changes).

"time changes".

Physical meaning – Symbol of change and the dynamism of life. This symbol informs us about the dynamism of space and time. Although space appears inactive it is bent by heavy and accelerated objects.

Metaphysical meaning – Space is real. Time is an allusion. The most important thing is the Now. The past, present, and future all exist in the now. Symbolize constancy of action and deeds.

15.Mpatapɔ

Original Adinkra Symbol:

Adinkra Alphabet – M/m

Numerical value – 90

Literal meaning: Mpata (Reconciliation), pɔ (Knot).

"Knot of pacification/reconciliation".

Physical meaning – Represent the bond or knot that binds parties in a dispute to a peaceful, harmonious reconciliation.

Metaphysical meaning – Symbol of reconciliation, peacemaking, and pacification.

16.Nkyimu

Original Adinkra Symbol:

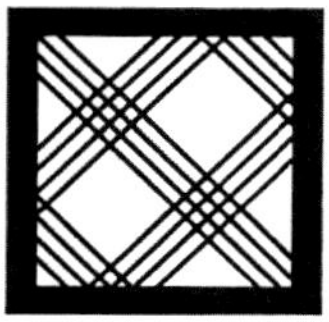

Adinkra Alphabet – N/n

Numerical value – 100

Literal meaning: Nkyimu (Divider).

"The crossed divisions made on adinkra cloth before stamping".

Physical meaning – Before adinkra cloth is stamped with the symbols, the artisan blocks off the cloth with lines in a rectangular grid using a broad-tooth comb. This preparation is symbolic of the exacting technique which results in the highest quality product.

Metaphysical meaning – Symbolize skillfulness and precision.

17.Pempamsie

Original Adinkra Symbol:

Adinkra Alphabet – P/p

Numerical value – 2.

Literal meaning: Pempam- (Sew), Sie (Preserve).

“Sew to preserve”.

Physical meaning – preparedness and readiness.

Metaphysical meaning – Understanding.

18.Denkyɛm

Original Adinkra Symbol:

Adinkra Alphabet – Q/q

Numerical value – 8

Literal meaning: Denkyɛm (Crocodile).

"Crocodile".

Physical meaning –We should learn to adjust to different situations in life.

Metaphysical meaning – There is nothing constant except change. We should adapt to changing conditions in our life and the environment.

19.Asase Ye Duru

Original Adinkra Symbol:

Adinkra Alphabet – R/r

Numerical value – 200

Literal meaning: Asase (Earth), Duru (Heavy).

"The Earth has weight". The earth exerts gravitational pull on all objects around it.

Physical meaning – The importance of the Earth in sustaining life. Heavy and accelerated objects bend space.

Metaphysical meaning – Symbolizes the providence and divinity of Mother Earth.

20.Sankɔfa

Original Adinkra Symbol:

Adinkra Alphabet – S/s

Numerical value – 1.

Literal meaning: San (Go back), Kɔfa (Take).

"Go back and take".

Physical meaning – Bringing past useful experiences into the present.

Metaphysical meaning – Wisdom. Learning from the past to build the future. Ancient wisdom from our past can help guide our way forward.

21. Aya

Original Adinkra Symbol:

Adinkra Alphabet – T/t

Numerical value – 300

Literal meaning – Aya (Fern).

"Fern".

Physical meaning: The fern is hardy plant that can grow in difficult places.

Symbolizes an individual who has endured many adversities and outlasted much difficulty.

Metaphysical meaning – Symbolizes endurance and resourcefulness.

22.Bese Saka

Original Adinkra Symbol:

Adinkra Alphabet – V/v

Numerical value – 400

Literal meaning: Bese (Cola nuts) Saka (Sack).

"Sack of cola nuts".

Physical meaning – Symbolizes the role of agriculture and trade in bringing people together.

Metaphysical meaning – Symbolizes Affluence, Power, Abundance, Plenty, Togetherness and Unity.

23. Wawa Aba

Original Adinkra Symbol:

Adinkra Alphabet – W/w

Numerical value – 500

Literal meaning: Wawa (Wawa tree), Aba (Seed).

"Seed of the Wawa tree".

Physical meaning – The seed of the Wawa tree is extremely hard. It inspires the individual to persevere through hardship.

Metaphysical meaning – Symbolizes Hardiness and Perseverance.

24.Akokɔnan

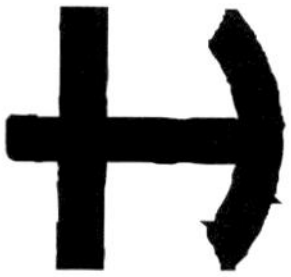

Original Adinkra Symbol:

Adinkra Alphabet – X/x

Numerical value – 600

Literal meaning: Akokɔ (Hen), Nan (Leg).

"The leg of a hen".

Physical meaning – The ideal nature of parenting is both protective and corrective.

Metaphysical meaning – Symbolizes Nurturing and Discipline.

25.Duafe

Original Adinkra Symbol:

Adinkra Alphabet – Y/y

Numerical value – 700

Literal meaning: Dua (Wooden), Fe (Comb),

"Wooden comb".

Physical meaning – Symbolizes desirable feminine qualities.

Metaphysical meaning – Symbol of Beauty and Cleanliness.

26.Fihankra

Original Adinkra Symbol:

Adinkra Alphabet – Z/z

Numerical value – 800

Literal meaning: Fi- (left), ha (here),

ankra (no goodbye).

"You did not say goodbye when you left home".

Physical meaning – Symbol to invite Africans in the diaspora who were sold into slavery to return home. Symbol reflect Akan's concept of family and depicts a kind of Akan architecture.

Metaphysical meaning – Symbolizes Security and Safety.

Special Characters - Akan

27.Dwennimmɛn

Original Adinkra Symbol:

Adinkra Alphabet – Ɛ/ɛ

Numerical value – 10

Literal meaning: Dwennim (Ram) Mɛn (Horns).

"ram's horns".

Physical meaning – The ram will fight fiercely against an adversary, but it also submits humbly to slaughter, emphasizing that even the strong needs to be humble.

Metaphysical meaning – Symbolizes humility together with strength. It also symbolizes resilience.

28.Ɔsram Ne Nsoromma

Original Adinkra Symbol:

Adinkra Alphabet – Ɔ/ɔ

Numerical value - 900

Literal meaning: Ɔsram (Moon), Nsoromma (Star).

"The Moon and the Star".

Physical meaning - This symbol reflects the harmony that exists in the bonding between a man and a woman.

Metaphysical meaning – Symbolizes love, faithfulness, and harmony.

Special Characters – Ewe

29.Funtunfunefu Dɛnkyɛmfunefu

Original Adinkra Symbol:

Adinkra Alphabet – Ɖ/ɖ

Numerical value – 7,000

Literal Meaning: Denkyɛm (crocodile),

Funtunfune (Conjoined).

"Conjoined Crocodiles".

Physical Meaning – Symbolizes the importance of working together and avoiding tribalism and racism.

Metaphysical Meaning – Democracy and unity in diversity.

30.Mpuanum

Original Adinkra Symbol:

Adinkra Alphabet – Dz/dz

Numerical value – 5,000

Literal Meaning: Mpua (tufts), anum (five).

"Five tufts of hair".

Physical Meaning – This is the traditional coded hairstyle of priestesses and is said to be the hairstyle of joy.

Metaphysical Meaning – Symbolize loyalty and skillfulness.

31.Hye Wonhye

Original Adinkra Symbol:

Adinkra Alphabet – Ƒ/ƒ

Numerical value – 1,000

Literal Meaning: Hye (burn), Wonhye (You do not burn).

"That which cannot be burnt".

Physical Meaning – The ability to withstand hardship and life difficulties.

Metaphysical Meaning - Symbolizes imperishability and endurance.

32. Mate Masie

Original Adinkra Symbol:

Adinkra Alphabet – Gb/gb

Numerical value – 11,000

Literal Meaning: Mate (I hear), Masie (I keep).

"What I hear, I keep".

Physical Meaning – Symbolizes receptivity to learning and education.

Metaphysical Meaning – Prudence.

33.Ɔkɔdeɛ Mmɔwerɛ

Original Adinkra Symbol:

Adinkra Alphabet – Ɣ/ɣ

Numerical value – 9,000

Literal Meaning: Ɔkɔdeɛ (Eagle), Mmɔwerɛ (Talon).

"The Talons of the eagle".

Physical Meaning – Symbolizes strength in unity.

Metaphysical Meaning – Symbolizes strength and power.

34.Nyansapɔ

Original Adinkra Symbol:

Adinkra Alphabet – Kp/kp

Numerical value – 3,000

Literal Meaning: Nyansa (Wisdom), pɔ (Knot).

"Wisdom knot".

Physical Meaning – Symbolizes the power and skill found in wise and intelligent sayings such as proverbs.

Metaphysical Meaning – Symbol of wisdom and intelligence.

35.Nsaa

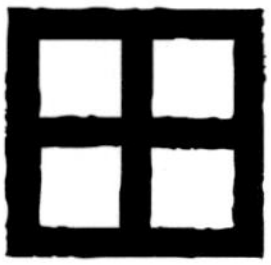

Original Adinkra Symbol:

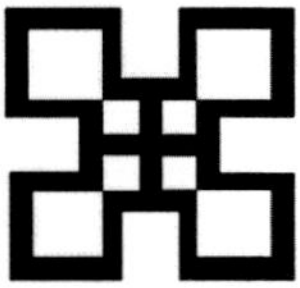

Adinkra Alphabet – Ny/ny

Numerical value – 4,000

Literal Meaning: Nsaa (High quality hand-woven fabric made in Bandiagara, the largest village in ancient Dogon country).

Physical Meaning – Symbolizes quality and durability.

Metaphysical Meaning – Symbolizes excellence and authenticity.

36.Akoma

Original Adinkra Symbol:

Adinkra Alphabet - Ʊ/ʊ

Numerical value – 6,000

Literal Meaning: Akoma (heart).

“The heart”.

Physical Meaning – Symbolizes love, goodwill, patience, faithfulness, endurance, and consistency.

Metaphysical Meaning – Symbol of Love.

37.Nyame Nwu Na Mawu.

Original Adinkra Symbol:

Adinkra Alphabet – Ts/ts

Numerical value – 2,000

Literal Meaning: Nyame (God), Nwu (never die),

Na (and) Mawu (I cannot die) "God does not die, and so I cannot die".

Physical Meaning – The spirit of God, (the soul) lives in me and therefore I cannot die. I am an expression of the Divine.

Metaphysical Meaning – Symbolizes Immortality of the soul.

Special Characters – Ga

38.Nkɔnsɔnkɔnsɔn

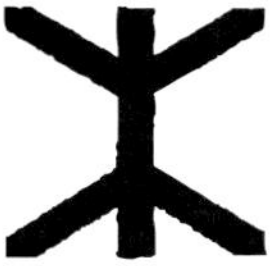

Original Adinkra Symbol:

Adinkra Alphabet – Ŋ/ ŋ

Numerical value – 8,000

Literal Meaning: Nkɔnsɔnkɔnsɔn – (chain).

"Chain or Link".

Physical Meaning – Symbolizes Interdependence, brotherhood, and cooperation.

Metaphysical Meaning – Symbolizes Unity and Responsibility.

Special Characters – Dagbani.

39.Mframadan

Original Adinkra Symbol:

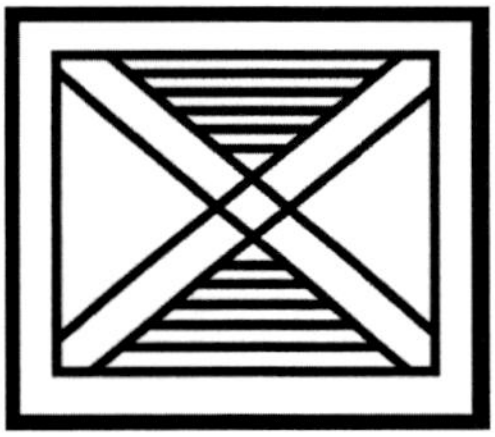

Adinkra Alphabet – Ch/ch

Numerical value – 10,000

Literal Meaning: mframa (wind), Dan (house).

"Wind-resistant house".

Physical Meaning – Symbolize social security, excellence, and preparedness.

Metaphysical Meaning – Symbolize Fortitude.

40. Kɛtɛ Pa

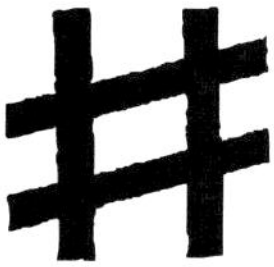

Original Adinkra Symbol:

Adinkra Alphabet – Sh/sh

Numerical value – 13,000

Literal Meaning: kɛtɛ (bed), pa (good).

“good bed”.

Physical Meaning – Symbol of faithfulness.

Metaphysical Meaning – Symbolize faith, love, and hope.

41.Nkyinkyim

Original Adinkra Symbol:

Adinkra Alphabet – Ʒ/ ʒ

Numerical value – 12,000

Literal Meaning: Nkyinkyim (twisting's).

"Twisting".

Physical Meaning – Symbol of toughness, adaptability, and ability to withstand hardships.

Metaphysical Meaning – Symbolize adaptability.

Special Characters – Astronomy

42.Nsoromma

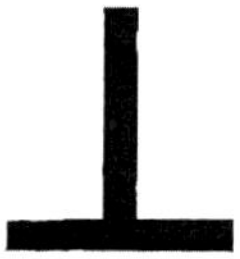

Original Adinkra Symbol:

Adinkra Alphabet – None.

Numerical value – 14,000

Literal Meaning: Soro (heavens), mma (child).

“A child of the heavens” or “a star”.

Physical Meaning – Symbol of a person who is a leader or a guardian.

Metaphysical Meaning – Symbolize giving or guardianship.

43.Ɔsram

Original Adinkra Symbol:

Adinkra Alphabet – None.

Numerical value – 15,000

Literal Meaning: Ɔsram (moon).

"The Moon".

Physical Meaning – Symbol of faith, patience, silence and understanding.

Metaphysical Meaning – Silence.

44.Boa Me Na Me Mmoa Wo

Original Adinkra Symbol:

Adinkra Alphabet – None.

Numerical value – 16,000

Literal Meaning: Boa (help), Me (me) Na (and)

Wo (you).

"Help me and let me help you".

Physical Meaning – Symbol of Cooperation and Interdependence.

Metaphysical Meaning – Cooperation.

45.Ɔdɔ Nyera Fie Kwan

Original Adinkra Symbol:

Adinkra Alphabet – None.

Numerical value – 17,000

Literal Meaning: Ɔdɔ - (love), Nyera/nnyew – (never loses), Fie (home), kwan (path).

"Love never loses its way home".

Physical Meaning – Symbolize love, devotion, hope and faithfulness.

Metaphysical Meaning – Symbolize Hope.

46.Fofo

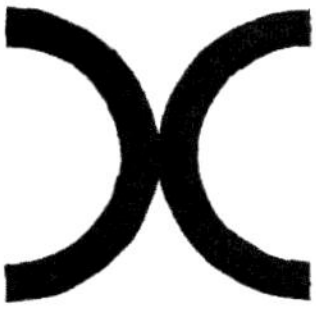

Original Adinkra Symbol:

Adinkra Alphabet – None.

Numerical value – 18,000

Literal Meaning: Fofo plant (botanical name – bidens pilosa).

"Seeds of fofo plant"

Physical Meaning – Symbol of warning against jealousy and covetousness. Fofo plant has a flower with yellow center and white petals. When the flower drops, they turn into black spiky-like seeds.

Metaphysical Meaning – Advises us that through Transmutation we should change negative aspects of our life into positive ones.

47.1 Akoben

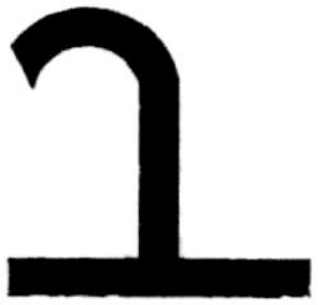

Original Adinkra Symbol:

Akoben

Adinkra Alphabet – None.

Numerical value – 19,000

Literal Meaning: Ako (war), ben (horn).

"War horn".

Physical Meaning – Symbolize a battle call to action. Meaning synonymous with Akofena.

Metaphysical Meaning – Symbolizes Courage.

47.2 Akofena

Original Adinkra Symbol:

Adinkra Alphabet – None.

Numerical value – 19,000

Literal Meaning: Ako (war), fena (sword).

"The state ceremonial swords".

Physical Meaning – Symbolize state authority and legality. Meaning synonymous with Akoben.

Metaphysical Meaning – Symbolizes Courage.

48.1 Gyawu Atikɔ

Original Adinkra Symbol:

Adinkra Alphabet – None.

Numerical value – 20,000

Literal Meaning: Gyawu (Bantamahene or Kumasi Krontihene (the commander in Chief of Kumasi army),

Atikɔ (back of the head).

"Shaving on the back of Gyawu's head".

Physical Meaning – Symbolize a brave person who attends to the Asante King. Meaning synonymous with Kwatakye Atikɔ

Metaphysical Meaning – Bravery/Honor.

48.2 Kwatakye Atikɔ

Original Adinkra Symbol:

Adinkra Alphabet – None.

Numerical value – 20,000

Literal Meaning: Kwatakye – (an Asante War Captain), atikɔ (the back of the head).

"Special hair style of Kwatakye, a war captain of old Asante".

Physical Meaning – Symbolize a brave person or a valiant man. Meaning synonymous with Gyawu Atikɔ.

Metaphysical Meaning – Bravery/Honor.

49.Musuyideɛ

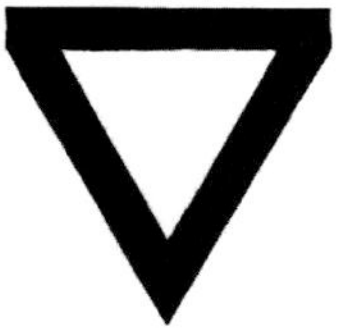

Original Adinkra Symbol:

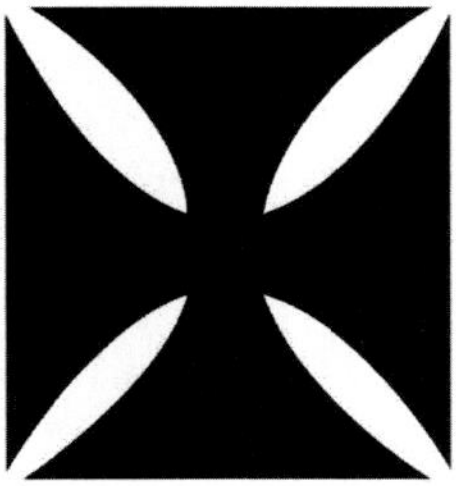

Adinkra Alphabet – None.

Numerical value – 21,000

Literal Meaning: Musu (evil), yi (remove), deɛ (thing).

"Thing to remove evil".

Physical Meaning – Talisman that is used to ward off negativity.

Metaphysical Meaning – Symbolizes sanctity, good fortune, and enlightenment. He that holds the ATOL (Adinkra Tree of Life)/AFOL (Adinkra Flower of Life) or Ankh wears the Mmusuyideɛ.

50.Owuo Atwedeɛ

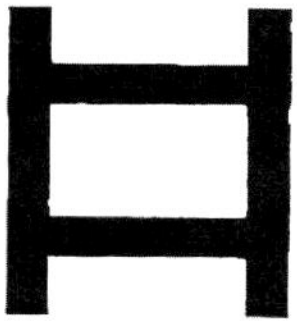

Original Adinkra Symbol:

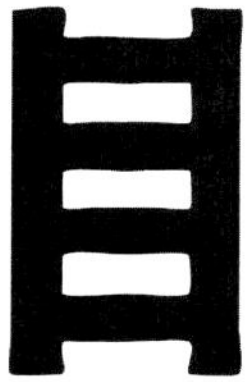

Adinkra Alphabet – None.

Numerical value – 22,000

Literal Meaning: Owuo (death), Atwedeɛ (ladder).

"The ladder of death".

Physical Meaning – This goes with the saying "The ladder of death will be climbed by all". Symbolizes the mortal aspect of our being including emotions, genetics, the physical body, electromagnetic forces and atoms.

Metaphysical Meaning – Symbolizes mortality, the physical body and spirit.

51.Sunsum

Original Adinkra Symbol:

Adinkra Alphabet – None.

Numerical value – 23,000

Literal Meaning: Sunsum (soul).

The "Soul".

Physical Meaning – Symbolizes cleanliness of spirit and spirituality. The soul is the aspect of The Creator or God in man/woman and it is perfect.

Metaphysical Meaning – Symbolizes immortality, the Metaphysical body and Soul.

52.Nyame Dua

Original Adinkra Symbol:

Adinkra Alphabet – None.

Numerical value – 24,000

Literal Meaning: Nyame (God), Dua (Tree).

"Tree of God".

Physical Meaning – Sacred altar of God. Signifies the presence and protection of God.

Metaphysical Meaning – Represents Eternal life, Adinkra Tree of life (ATOL) and Adinkra Flower of life (AFOL). It is synonymous with the Egyptian Ankh. Symbolize deeper knowledge of the physical and metaphysical world.

Adinkra Alphabet Planetary and Cardinal signs Characters

Adinkra Alphabet	Numerical Value	Standard character	Simplified Character
Nsoromma	14000		
Ɔsram	15000		
Boa Me Na Me Mmoa Wo	16000		
Ɔdɔ Nyera Fie Kwan	17000		
Fofo	18000		
Akofena	19000		
Akoben	19000		

Adinkra Alphabet Planetary and Cardinal signs Characters

Adinkra Alphabet	Numerical Value	Standard character	Simplified Character
Kwatakye Atikɔ	20000		
Gyawu Atikɔ	20000		
Mmusuyideɛ	21000		
Owuo Atwedeɛ	22000		
Sunsum	23000		
Nyame Dua	24000		

ADINKRA ALPHABET

a b c d e
f g h i j
k l m n o
p q r s t
u v w x y
z ɛ ɔ

Adinkra Alphabet

ADINKRA ALPHABET

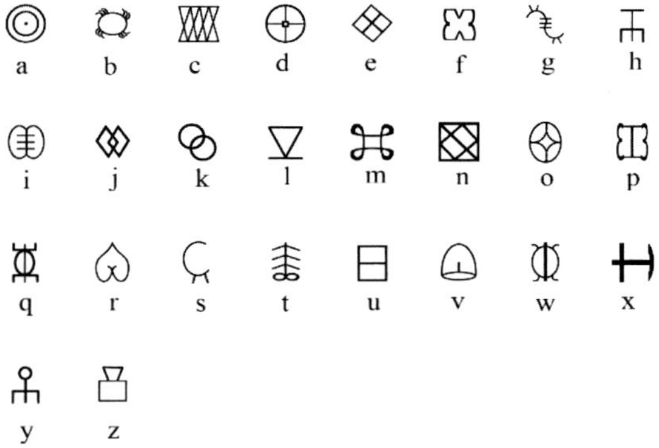
a b c d e f g h
i j k l m n o p
q r s t u v w x
y z

SPECIAL CHARACTERS FOR AKAN, EWE, GA AND DAGBANI

ch ɖ dz ɛ ƒ gb ɣ kp
ny ŋ ɔ sh ts ʋ ʒ

ADINKRA ALPHABET

AKAN, EWE, GA AND DAGBANI

1. Adinkrahene (A/a)
2. Bi Nka Bi (B/b)
3. Ɔwɔ Foro Adobɛ (C/c)
4. Dame-Dame (D/d)
5. Ɛban (E/e)
6. Fawohodie (F/f)
7. Gye Nyame (G/g)
8. Hwemudua (H/h)
9. Ɛse Ne Tɛkrɛma (I/i)
10. Ɛpa (J/j)
11. Kintinkantan (K/k)
12. Mmerɛ Dane (L/l)
13. Mpatapɔ (M/m)
14. Nkyimu (N/n)
15. Nyame Biribi Wɔ Soro (O/o)
16. Pempamsie (P/p)
17. Dɛnkyɛm (Q/q)
18. Asase Ye Duru (R/r)
19. Sankɔfa (S/s)
20. Aya (T/t)
21. Nea Onnim No Sua A, Ohu (U/u)
22. Bese Saka (V/v)
23. Wawa Aba (W/w)
24. Akokɔnan (X/x)
25. Duafe (Y/y)
26. Fihankra (Z/z)
27. Mframadan (Ch/ch)
28. Funtunfunefu - Dɛnkyɛmfunefu (Đ/ɖ)
29. Mpuanum (Dz/dz)
30. Dwennimmɛn (Ɛ/ɛ)
31. Hye Wonhye (Ƒ/ƒ)
32. Mate Masie (Gb/gb)
33. Ɔkɔdeɛ Mmɔwerɛ (Ɣ/ɣ)
34. Nyansapɔ (Kp/kp)
35. Nsaa (Ny/ny)
36. Nkɔnsɔnkɔnsɔn (Ŋ/ŋ)
37. Ɔsram Ne Nsoromma (Ɔ/ɔ)
38. Kɛtɛ Pa (Sh/sh)
39. Nyame Nnwu Na Mawu (Ts/ts)
40. Akoma (Ʊ/ʊ)
41. Nkyinkyim (Ʒ/ʒ)
42. Nyame Dua

ADINKRA ALPHABET

(Simplified)

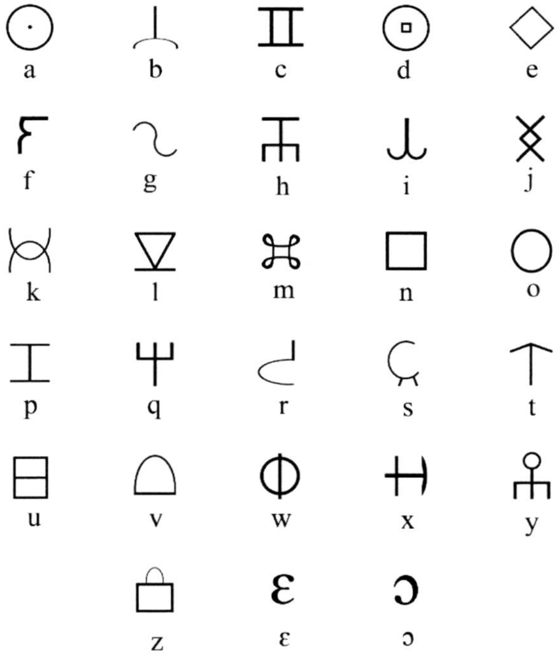
a b c d e
f g h i j
k l m n o
p q r s t
u v w x y
z ɛ ɔ

ADINKRA ALPHABET

(Akan, Ewe, Ga and Dagbani-Simplified)

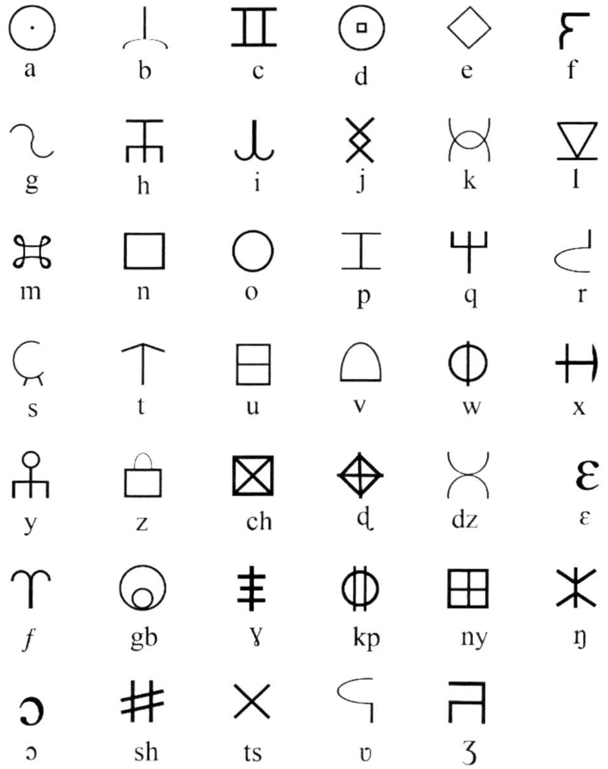
a b c d e f
g h i j k l
m n o p q r
s t u v w x
y z ch ɖ dz ɛ
ƒ gb ɣ kp ny ŋ
ɔ sh ts ʋ ʒ

ADINKRA ALPHABET

Akan, Ewe, Ga and Dagbani

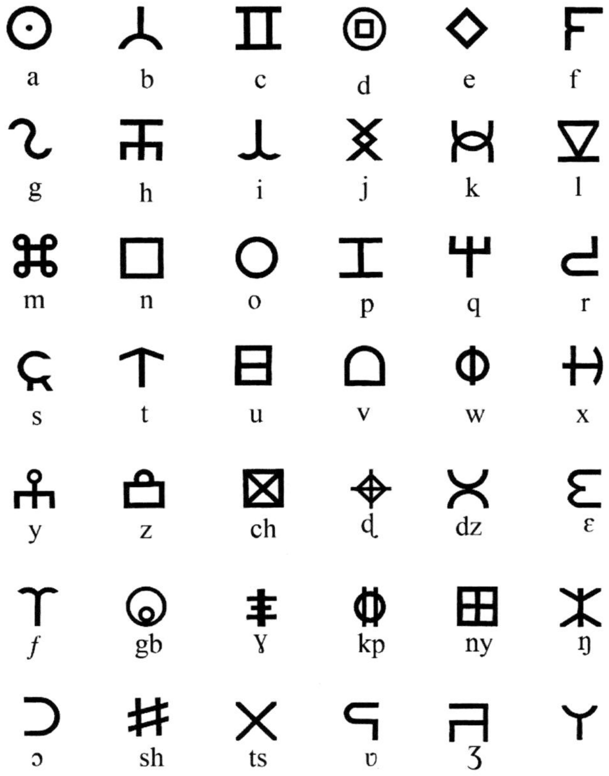
a b c d e f
g h i j k l
m n o p q r
s t u v w x
y z ch ɖ dz ɛ
ƒ gb ɣ kp ny ŋ
ɔ sh ts ʋ ʒ

Adinkra Tree of Life

The Tree of Life is a Kabbalistic metaphysical symbol consisting of 10 pathways of virtue or vortices of energy known as the Sephirot. In Kabbalah the Sephirot is a symbol of creation and how the universe came into being starting from top of the Tree of Life to the bottom. The ten Sephirot corresponds with the 10 regions of sound production as explained in the phonetic section. From below to above it represents a pathway of virtues consisting of two pillars with a middle pathway that the individual must travel to reach God or the Creator. The Adinkra Tree of Life follows the same principles but the Sephirot consist of Adinkra symbols or Adinkra alphabet.

The Adinkra tree of life (ATOL) is a pathway of virtues that lead to greater understanding of God or the Creator. It consists of two columns with a middle pathway. Each of the pathways start with Fawohodie or freedom as the foundation. The observer views the tree standing behind it with the right column on the left side of the page and the left column on the right side of the page.

The middle pathway shows that through freedom, adaptability and aiming for something higher we can gain a greater understanding of God and the Self.

The right and left column are two opposite polarities: masculine and feminine, yin and yang, positive and negative respectively.

The right column or positive polarity shows that through freedom, steadfastness and experience we can attain the Greater Light and gain understanding of The Creator.

The left column, which is the negative pole shows that through freedom, hard work, applying the right judgment and understanding we can attain understanding of the Creator.

All three pathways on the Adinkra Tree of Life ultimately lead to Gye Nyame which is The Greater Light ("Dark Energy-Dark Matter") or God the Creator. In creation The Greater Light or "Dark Energy-Dark Matter" manifested through the other nine vortices of energy to form the universe.

Symbols were assigned on the tree based on their metaphysical meaning and their similarity to the Sephirot they represent. Gye Nyame is the Greater Light or "Dark Energy-Dark Matter" and synonymous with the Crown of the Tree. Wisdom is gained from experience in going back (Sankɔfa) for that which is good. There is understanding in preserving that which is good (Pempamsie). The Universe was created (Adinkrahene) in Mercy. A prudent (Dame-Dame) life of service will benefit an individual and society.

One must aim higher (Nyame Biribi Wo Soro) for a better and beautiful world. Knowledge (Nea Onnim No Sua A, Ohu) is splendid. Victory is attained by overcoming your difficulties (Owo Foro Adobe). The world and things around us are always changing but we should learn to be grounded in constancy (Denkyem). Freedom (Fawohodie) is the beginning of life.

Knowledge is attained through meditation and contemplation on the tree of life (Nyame Dua).

The relationship between Adinkra Alphabet, Adinkra Tree of Life (ATOL) and Adinkra Numerology is easily demonstrated on the Adinkra Flower of Life (AFOL) (page 99,100).

The 11 spheres on the ATOL is related to the 11 dimensions of space in quantum physics. Each sphere is also associated with a musical note. The note of the three higher spheres is too high for the human ear. The association of the lower spheres and music note is as shows on the table below (Page #94).

Adinkra number	Kabbalah number	Adinkra name	Kabbalistic name
0	1	Gye Nyame	Crown
1	2	Sankɔfa	Wisdom
2	3	Pempamsie	Understanding
3	4	Adinkrahene	Mercy
4	5	Dame-Dame	Severity
5	6	Nyame Biribi Wɔ Soro	Beauty
6	7	Ɔwo Foro Adobɛ	Victory
7	8	Nea Onnim No Sua A, Ohu	Splendor
8	9	Denkyɛm	Foundation
9	10	Fawohodie	Kingdom

Adinkra sphere	Kabbalah sphere	Musical note	Musical sound
Adinkrahene	Mercy	C	Do
Dame Dame	Severity	D	Re
Nyame Biribi Wɔ Soro	Beauty	E	Mi
Ɔwɔ Foro Adobɛ	Victory	F	Fa
Nea Onnim No Sua A Ohu	Splendor	G	Sol
Dɛnkyɛm	Foundation	A	La
Fawohodie	Kingdom	B	Tee

ADINKRA TREE OF LIFE

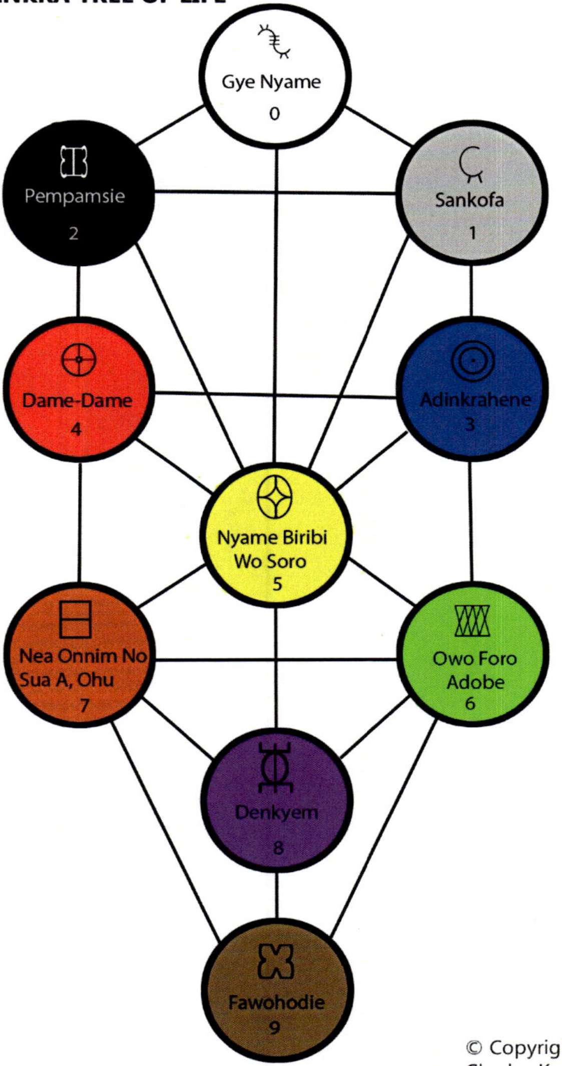
Gye Nyame
0
Pempamsie
2
Sankofa
1
Dame-Dame
4
Adinkrahene
3
Nyame Biribi Wo Soro
5
Nea Onnim No Sua A, Ohu
7
Owo Foro Adobe
6
Denkyem
8
Fawohodie
9

ADINKRA TREE OF LIFE

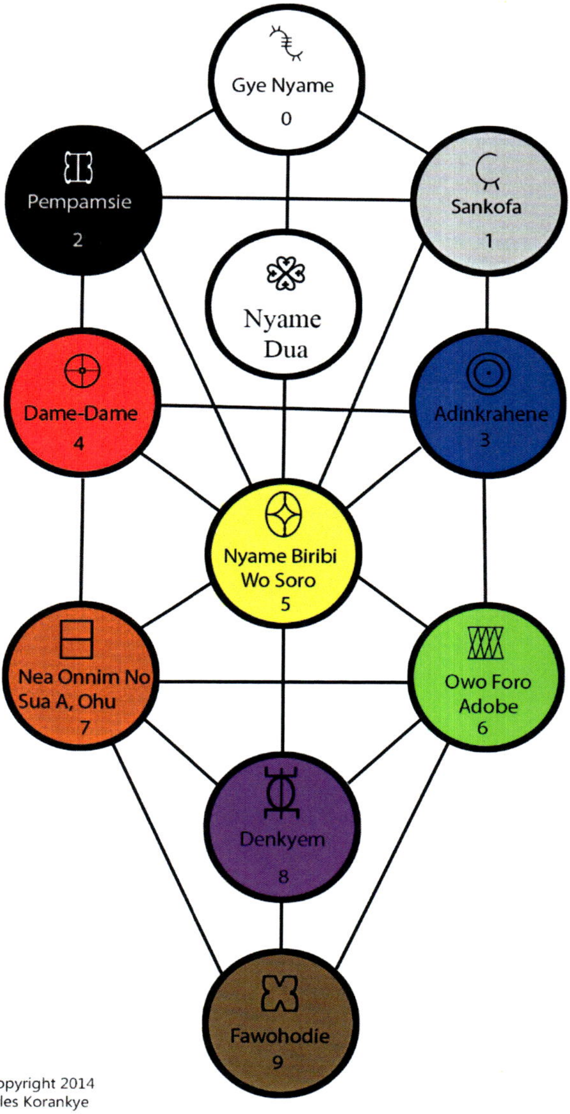
Gye Nyame
0
Pempamsie
2
Sankofa
1
Nyame
Dua
Dame-Dame
4
Adinkrahene
3
Nyame Biribi
Wo Soro
5
Nea Onnim No
Sua A, Ohu
7
Owo Foro
Adobe
6
Denkyem
8
Fawohodie
9

Adinkra Flower of Life

The Adinkra Flower of Life (AFOL) is a pathway through consciousness that leads to a deeper understanding of self, the universe and all the dimensions of space. The AFOL consist of three Adinkra Tree of Life (ATOL) joined at the center by Gye Nyame sphere. Each tree on the AFOL leads to Gye Nyame or the Greater Light. The uniqueness of the AFOL compare to other variations of the Kabballistic Tree of Life arose from asigning zero to the crown sphere or Gye Nyame. The trees on the AFOL are named right arm, middle arm and left arm. The right arm tree represent the physical aspect of nature. The left arm tree represent the emotional aspect of nature and the middle arm represent the metaphysical aspect of nature.

There is one unmanifested tree that is not shown. The unmanifested tree is link to Nyame Dua, which is an entry point that exist between our world and higher dimensions of space.

The AFOL must be viewed as a tetrahedron with the three trees and as a pyramid when the unmanifested tree is added. In this sense there are manifested world which is the one we exist in and unmanifested world which is at the higher dimensions and it is the world that we transition into after death. The unmanifested world has the same spheres as the manifest world but in our current state of consciousness as living beings we are unable to fully comprehend it.

The AFOL has a total of 100 characters. This consist of 28 spheres, 22 paths x 3 = 66, one sphere of Nyame Dua x 3 and one sphere of Kɛtɛ Pa x 3.

The unmanifested world is under the rulership of Nyame Dua and the manifested world is under the rulership of Gye Nyame. The manifested world consist of the physical world and the metaphysical world. The physical world is under the rulership of Sunsum and the metaphysical world is under the rulership of Kɛtɛ Pa. Gye Nyame, Nyame Dua, Sunsum and Kɛtɛ Pa represent one and the same Energy source, The Greater Light or "Dark Energy-Dark Matter". The unmanifested Energy is Dark Energy-Dark Matter and the manifested form is the Greater Light.

Adinkra Flower of Life

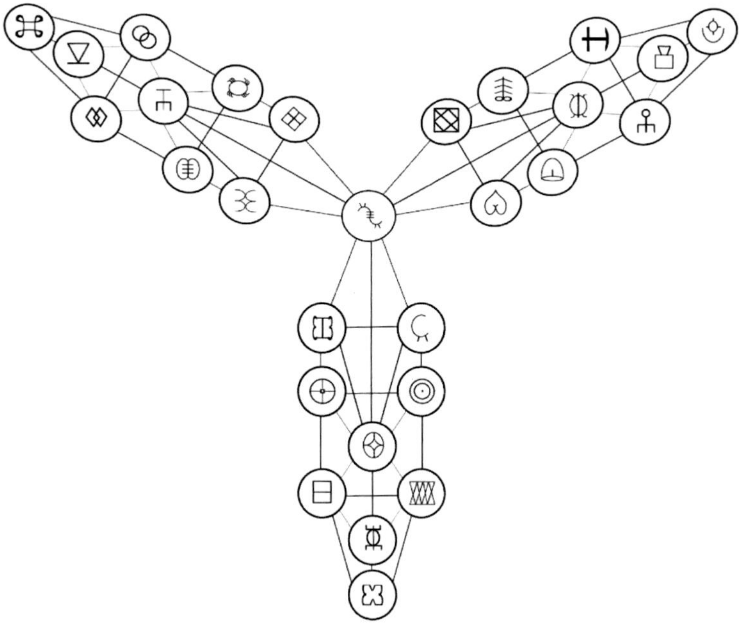

Adinkra Flower of Life

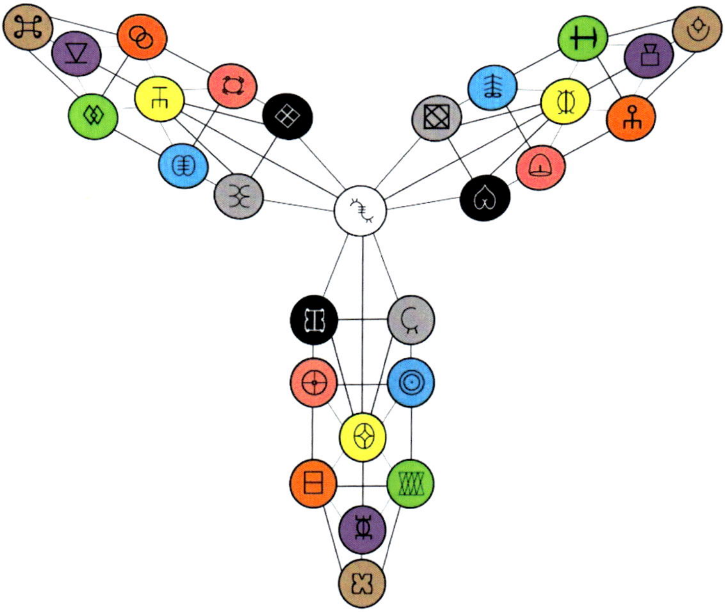

Adinkra Virtues

No.	Adinkra	Virtue
1	Adinkrahene	Mercy/Kindness
2	Bi Nka Bi	Peace
3	Ɔdɔ Foro Adobɛ	Victory
4	Dame Dame	Judgement
5	Ɛban	Charity
6	Fawohodie	Kingship
7	Gye Nyame	God
8	Hwemudua	Perfection
9	Ɛse Ne Tɛkrɛma	Unity
10	Ɛpa	Moderation
11	Kintinkantan	Humility
12	Mmerɛ Dane	Constancy
13	Mpatapɔ	Reconciliation
14	Nkyimu	Precision

No.	Adinkra	Virtue
15	Nyame Biribi Wɔ Soro	Beauty
16	Pempamsie	Understanding
17	Dɛnkyɛm	Foundation
18	Asase Ye Duru	Providence
19	Sankɔfa	Wisdom
20	Aya	Endurance
21	Nea Onnim No Sua A, Ohu	Service
22	Bese Saka	Resourcefulness
23	Wawa Aba	Perseverance
24	Akokɔnan	Discipline
25	Duafe	Cleanliness
26	Fihankra	Security
27	Dwennimmɛn	Resilience
28	Ɔsram Ne Nsoromma	Harmony

No.	Adinkra	Virtue
29	Hye Wonhye	Imperishability
30	Nyame Nnwu Na Mawu	Immortality
31	Nyansapɔ	Intelligence
32	Nsaa	Excellence
33	Mpuanum	Skillfulness
34	Akoma	Love
35	Funtunfunefu-Dɛnkyɛmfunefu	Diversity
36	Nkɔnsɔnkɔnsɔn	Responsibility
37	Ɔkɔdeɛ Mmɔwerɛ	Strength
38	Mframadan	Fortitude
39	Mate Masie	Prudence
40	Nkyinkyim	Adaptability
41	Kɛtɛ Pa	Faith
42	Nsoromma	Giving/ Guardianship

No.	Adinkra	Virtue
43	Ɔsram	Silence
44	Boa Me Na Me Mmoa Wo	Cooperation
45	Ɔdɔ Nyera Fie Kwan	Hope
46	Fofo	Transmutation
47	Akoben/ Akofena	Courage
48	Gyawu Atikɔ/ Kwatakye Atikɔ	Bravery/Honor
49	Mmusuyideɛ	Enlightenment
50	Owuo Atwedeɛ	Mortality/Spirit
51	Sunsum	Soul
52	Nyame Dua	Knowledge

Adinkra Numerology

No.	Adinkra	Numerical value	Alphabet
1	Gye Nyame	0	g
2	Sankɔfa	1	s
3	Pempamsie	2	p
4	Adinkrahene	3	a
5	Dame Dame	4	d
6	Nyame Biribi Wɔ Soro	5	o
7	Ɔwo Foro Adobɛ	6	c
8	Nea Onnim No Sua A, Ohu	7	u
9	Denkyɛm	8	q
10	Fahowodie	9	f
11	Dwennimmɛn	10	ɛ
12	Ɛban	20	b

No.	Adinkra	Numerical Value	Alphabet
13	Ɛse Ne Tɛkrɛma	30	e
14	Bi Nka Bi	40	b
15	Hwemudua	50	h
16	Ɛpa	60	j
17	Kintinkantan	70	k
18	Mmerɛ Dane	80	l
19	Mpatapɔ	90	m
20	Nkyimu	100	n
21	Asase Ye duru	200	r
22	Aya	300	t
23	Bese Saka	400	v
24	Wawa Aba	500	w
25	Akokɔnan	600	x
26	Duafe	700	y
27	Fihankra	800	z

No.	Adinkra	Numerical Value	Alphabet
28	Ɔsram Ne Nsoromma	900	ɔ
29	Hye Wonhye	1000	Ƒ/ƒ
30	Nyame Nnwu Na Mawu	2000	Ts/ts
31	Nyansapɔ	3000	Kp/kp
32	Nsaa	4000	Ny/ny
33	Mpuanum	5000	Dz/dz
34	Akoma	6000	Ʊ/ʊ
35	Funtunfunefu-Dɛnkyɛmfunefu	7000	Đ/ɖ
36	Nkɔnsɔnkɔnsɔn	8,000	Ŋ/ ŋ
37	Ɔkɔdeɛ Mmɔwerɛ	9,000	Ɣ/ɣ
38	Mframadan	10,000	Ch/ch
39	Mate Masie	11,000	Gb/gb
40	Nkyinkyim	12,000	Ʒ/ ʒ

No	Adinkra	Numerical value	Alphabet
41	Kɛtɛ Pa	13,000	Sh/sh
42	Nsoromma	14,000	None
43	Ɔsram	15,000	None
44	Boa Me Na Me Mmoa Wo	16,000	None
45	Ɔdɔ Nnyew Fie Kwan	17,000	None
46	Fofo	18,000	None
47	Akoben/Akofena	19,000	None
48	Gyawu Atikɔ/Kwatakye Atikɔ	20,000	None
49	Mmusuyideɛ	21,000	None
50	Owuo Atwedeɛ	22,000	None
51	Sunsum	23,000	None
52	Nyame Dua	24,000	None

Explanation of Numerology

Numbers 0 to 9 were selected based on their position on the Adinkra Tree of Life (ATOL). All the subsequent numbering in the Numerology Table can be derived from a combination of numbers between 0 and 9.

Dwennimmɛn was made number 10 for completion of the first ten symbols and Ɔsram Ne Nsoromma was assigned 900. The other letters were assigned numbers in order of tens and hundreds starting with the remaining vowels followed by the consonants. Characters on the pathway of the ATOL were assigned numbers starting with Hye Wonhye at 1000 and ending with Sunsum at 23,000. The highest assigned number is 24,000 and it is assigned to Nyame Dua. Nyame Dua is used as a number marker whenever necessary. Adinkra Alphabet character or characters written between two Nyame Dua characters should be read as a number.

Physical form implies that which is perceived by the five physical senses as in sight, hearing, taste, sensation, and smell. Metaphysical form implies that which involve abstract and concrete thought. Cosmic implies the total universe or multiverse and all the dimensions of space.

Geometrical Explanation of Numerology

Number	Composition	Geometry	Physical meaning	Metaphysical meaning
Zero, 0	0	Space	Limitless	Primordial/ infinite
One, 1	1	.	Dot	Physical form
Two, 2	2	——	line	Physical and Metaphysical form
Three, 3	1, 2	 ▲	Triangle	Physical Manifestation
Four, 4	2, 2	 ■	Square	Physical Stability
Five, 5	2, 3	 ⬠	Pentagon	Metaphysical Manifestation

Number	Composition	Geometry	Physical meaning	Metaphysical meaning
Six, 6	3, 3		Interlaced triangle	Physical and Metaphysical Manifestation
Seven, 7	3, 4		Interlaced triangle with dot	Metaphysical Stability
Eight, 8	4, 4		Two squares	Physical and Metaphysical Stability
Nine, 9	4, 5		Circle	Cosmic Manifestation
Ten, 10	5, 5		Circle with dot	Cosmic and Metaphysical Manifestation

Adinkra Alphabet Elemental properties

Adinkra alphabets are associated with 5 elements. The 5 elements are ether, air, fire, water, and earth. Ether is the unknown substance that compose Dark Energy and Dark Matter. There are four elements associated with Ether and they are Gye Nyame, Kɛtɛ Pa, Sunsum and Nyame Dua. There are 12 elements each in the remaining 4 groups. All the dimensions of space are divided into manifested and un-manifested. The manifested world is divided into physical and metaphysical world. The manifested world is ruled by Gye Nyame and the un-manifested world is ruled by Nyame Dua. The physical world is under the rulership of Sunsum, and the metaphysical world is under the rulership of Kɛtɛ Pa.

No	Adinkra	Element	Rulership
1	Gye Nyame	Ether	Manifested
2	Kɛtɛ Pa	Ether	Metaphysical
3	Sunsum	Ether	Physical
4	Nyame Dua	Ether	Un-manifested

No	Adinkra	Element
1	Nyame Biribi Wɔ Soro	Air
2	Dɛnkyɛm	Air
3	Hwemudua	Air
4	Mmerɛ Dane	Air
5	Wawa Aba	Air
6	Fihankra	Air
7	Nyansapɔ	Air
8	Funtunfunefu Dɛnkyɛmfunefu	Air
9	Mate Masie	Air
10	Musuyideɛ	Air
11	Boa Me Na Me Mmoa wo	Air
12	Nsoromma	Air
13	Sankofa	Fire
14	Dame Dame	Fire
15	Ɔwɔ Foro Adobɛ	Fire
16	Dwennimmɛn	Fire
17	Bi Nka Bi	Fire
18	Ɛpa	Fire
19	Nkyimu	Fire
20	Bese Saka	Fire
21	Akokɔnan	Fire
22	Hye Wonhye	Fire
23	Mpuanum	Fire
24	Ɔkɔdeɛ Mmɔwerɛ	Fire

No	Adinkra	Element
25	Pempamsie	Water
26	Adinkrahene	Water
27	Nea Onnim No sua A Ohu	Water
28	Ɛban	Water
29	Ɛse Ne Tɛkrɛma	Water
30	Kintinkantan	Water
31	Asase Ye Duru	Water
32	Aya	Water
33	Duafe	Water
34	Nsaa	Water
35	Nkɔnsɔnkɔnsɔn	Water
36	Nkyinkyim	Water
37	Fawohodie	Earth
38	Mpatapɔ	Earth
39	Ɔsram Ne Nsoromma	Earth
40	Nyame Nnwu Na Mawu	Earth
41	Akoma	Earth
42	Mframadan	Earth
43	Fofo	Earth
44	Akofena	Earth
45	Ɔdɔ Nyera Fie Kwan	Earth
46	Kwatakye Atikɔ	Earth
47	Ɔsram	Earth
48	Owuo Atwedeɛ	Earth

Rules for Assigning Elemental Properties

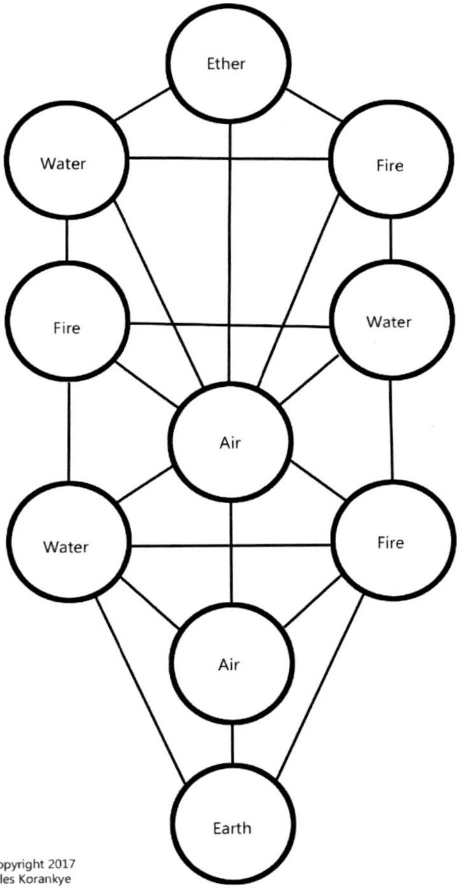
Ether
Water
Fire
Fire
Water
Air
Water
Fire
Air
Earth

Triplicity Rulership

Fire – Aries, Leo, Sagittarius

Earth – Taurus, Virgo, Capricorn

Air – Gemini, Libra, Aquarius

Water – Cancer, Scorpio, Pisces

Assignment of Elemental properties is based on the location of the character on the ATOL and correspondingly on AFOL as demonstrated on the diagram above. For the zodiac characters, the traditional classical astrological assignment based on triplicity rulership was maintained as above. The planetary characters were assigned to Earth with the exception of the Sun, Saturn and Mercury due to their traditional special properties. Sun, Saturn, and Mercury were all assigned to air.

Table of Colors and their Symbology

Color	Akan	Metaphysical Meaning
Black	Tuntum	Primordial color. The original and stable state of infinite energy and knowledge.
Darkness	Esum	Ignorance/Abyss
Blue	Bibire	Nature
Brown	Dɔdoe	Earth
Green	Ahabammono	Plant
Grey/Ash	Nsonso	Transition from Black to white
Red	Kɔkɔɔ	Blood
White	Fufuo/Fitaa	The expression of infinite energy and knowledge.
Yellow	Akokɔsradeɛ	Wealth
Orange	Ankaa	Nutrient
Gold	Sika	Natural money
Silver	Dwetɛ	Printed money
Purple	Beredum/ Ɔtankɔkɔɔ/ Afasebiri/ Afaseɛ	Royal
Pink	Memen	Blood line
Spotted	Nsisimu	Transformation

Adinkra Colors and their Meaning

The table above shows the Adinkra colors and their meaning. These colors correspond with the colors on the Adinkra Tree of Life (ATOL) and Adinkra Flower of Life (AFOL). Significant distinction is the difference and similarities between black and white. I have included darkness on the table although it is not a color as many people confuse darkness with black and use them interchangeably. Darkness is the absence of light and represent ignorance and the abyss. Black is the primordial state of matter. At this state light is absorbed. It is the state of silence. White on the other hand is the state of expression. At this state, all light is reflected. This can be illustrated with an atomic matter. The silent state of the matter where its energy is stable is the black state and the state where it releases its energy will be the white state. Essentially black and white can represent the same element depending on the behavior of the element or individual.

Adinkra Zodiac

No.	Adinkra	Zodiac	Numerical Value
1	Hye Wonhye	Aries	1000
2	Nyame Nnwu Na Mawu	Taurus	2000
3	Nyansapɔ	Gemini	3000
4	Nsaa	Cancer	4000
5	Mpuanum	Leo	5000
6	Akoma	Virgo	6000
7	Funtunfunefu - Dɛnkyɛmfunefu	Libra	7000
8	Nkɔnsɔnkɔnsɔn	Scorpio	8000
9	Ɔkɔdeɛ Mmɔwerɛ	Sagittarius	9000
10	Mframadan	Capricorn	10,000
11	Mate Masie	Aquarius	11,000
12	Nkyinkyim	Pisces	12,000
13	Kɛtɛ Pa	Ophiuchus	13,000

Adinkra Astronomy

No.	Adinkra	Astronomical Sign	Numerical Value
14	Nsoromma	Sun	14,000
15	Ɔsram	Moon	15,000
16	Boa Me Na Me Mmoa Wo	Mercury	16,000
17	Ɔdɔ Nyera Fie Kwan	Venus	17,000
18	Fofo	Earth	18,000
19	Akoben/ Akofena	Mars	19,000
20	Gyawu Atikɔ/ Kwatakye Atikɔ	Jupiter	20,000
21	Musuyideɛ	Saturn	21,000
22	Owuo Atwedeɛ	Uranus	22,000
23	Sunsum	Neptune	23,000

Adinkra Astronomical Sign and Day of the week Governed

Adinkra Name	Astronomical Sign	Day of Week
Nsoromma	Sun	Sunday
Ɔsram	Moon	Monday
Boa Me Na Me Mmoa Wo	Mercury	Wednesday
Ɔdɔ Nyera Fie Kwan	Venus	Friday
Fofo	Earth	None
Akoben/ Akofena	Mars	Tuesday
Gyawu Atikɔ/ Kwatakye Atikɔ	Jupiter	Thursday
Musuyideɛ	Saturn	Saturday
Owuo Atwedeɛ	Uranus	None
Sunsum	Neptune	None

Adinkra Astronomical Sign and Given Akan Names

Adinkra Name	Day of Week	Female	Male
Nsoromma	Sunday	Esi	Kwesi
Ɔsram	Monday	Adwoa	Kwadwo
Boa Me Na Me Mmoa Wo	Wednesday	Akua	Kwaku
Ɔdɔ Nyera Fie Kwan	Friday	Afua	Kofi
Fofo	N/A	N/A	N/A
Akoben/ Akofena	Tuesday	Abena	Kwabena
Gyawu Atikɔ/ Kwatakye Atikɔ	Thursday	Yaa	Yaw
Musuyideɛ	Saturday	Ama	Kwame
Owuo Atwedeɛ	N/A	N/A	N/A
Sunsum	N/A	N/A	N/A

Application of Adinkra Alphabet and Numbers

Below are the uses of the adinkra alphabet in writing and numbering. In the following pages adinkra alphabet is used to write Ghana patriotic songs in Akan, Ewe, Ga and Dagbani and the Ghana National Anthem in English. This is followed by the use of the adinkra alphabet in writing the 54 African countries. The adinkra numbering system shows the numbers one to hundred.

Adinkra Alphabet and numbers are also applicable to computer coding. In hexadecimal or base 16 computer coding using Adinkra Alphabets for numbers 10 to 15 and assigning characters from zero to 15 will result in characters for hexadecimal as 0, 1, 2, 3, 4, 5, 6, 7, 8, 9, ꝛ, ʢ, ⌶, ⊙, ◙, O. In this manner where the equal sign means assigned to, ϒꝛϒ = 10, ϒʢϒ = 11, ϒ⌶ϒ = 12, ϒ⊙ϒ = 13, ϒ◙ϒ = 14, and ϒOϒ = 15.

Ghana Patriotic Song-Akan

yɛn ara asaase

ni; ɛyɛ abɔɔden

de ma yɛn

mogya na

nananom hwie

gui, nya de

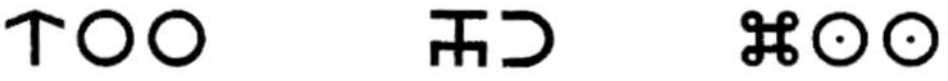

too hɔ maa

yɛn, aduru me

ne wo nso

so, sɛ

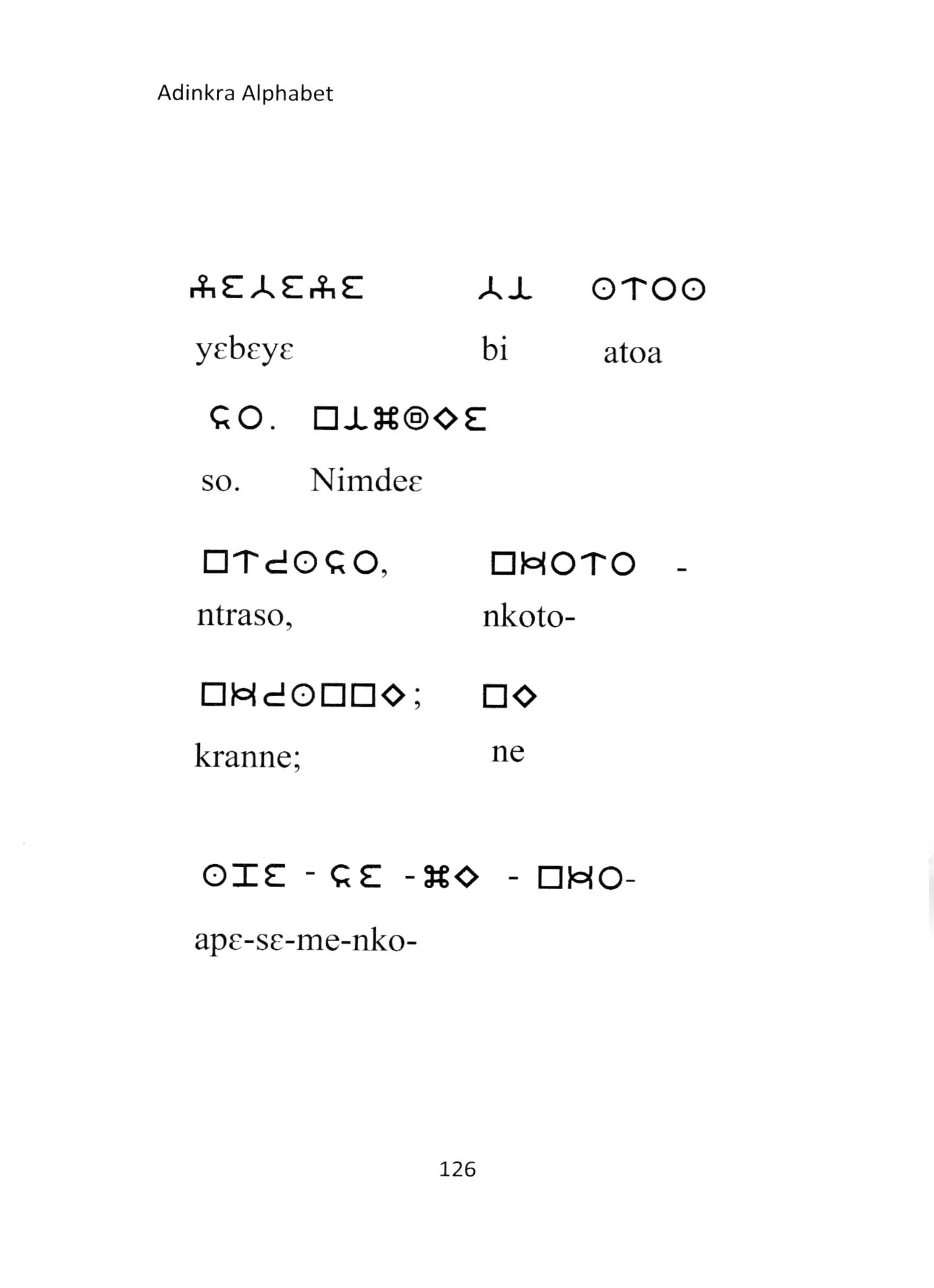

yɛbɛyɛ bi atoa

so. Nimdeɛ

ntraso, nkoto-

kranne; ne

apɛ-sɛ-me-nkomenya, adi yɛn

bra mu dɛm,

ma yɛn asaase

ho dɔ atomu sɛ.

⊃⌘⊙□ □O ϛƐ ,

ɔman no, sɛ

Ɛ⅄Ɛ♣Ɛ ♣⊥◇ O,

ɛbɛyɛ yie o,

⊃⌘⊙□ □O, ϛƐ

ɔman no, sɛ

Ɛ⊲◇□♣Ɛ ♣⊥◇ O;

ɛrenyɛ yie o;

ɛyɛ nsɛnnahɔ

sɛ, ɔmanfo

bra na

ɛkyerɛ.

Ghana National Anthem-English

God bless our

homeland

Ghana and

make our

nation great

and strong.

Bold to

defend

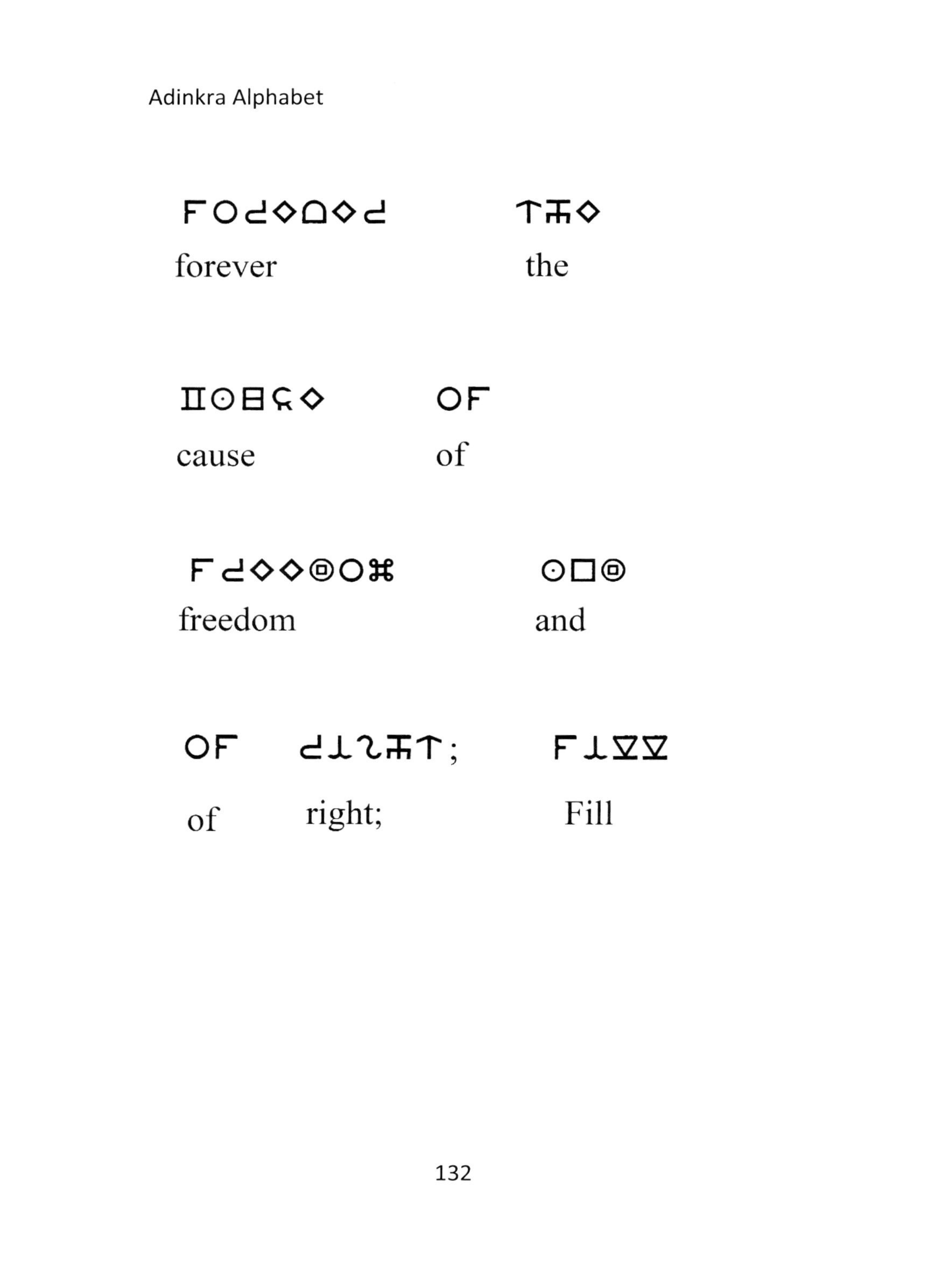

forever the

cause of

freedom and

of right; Fill

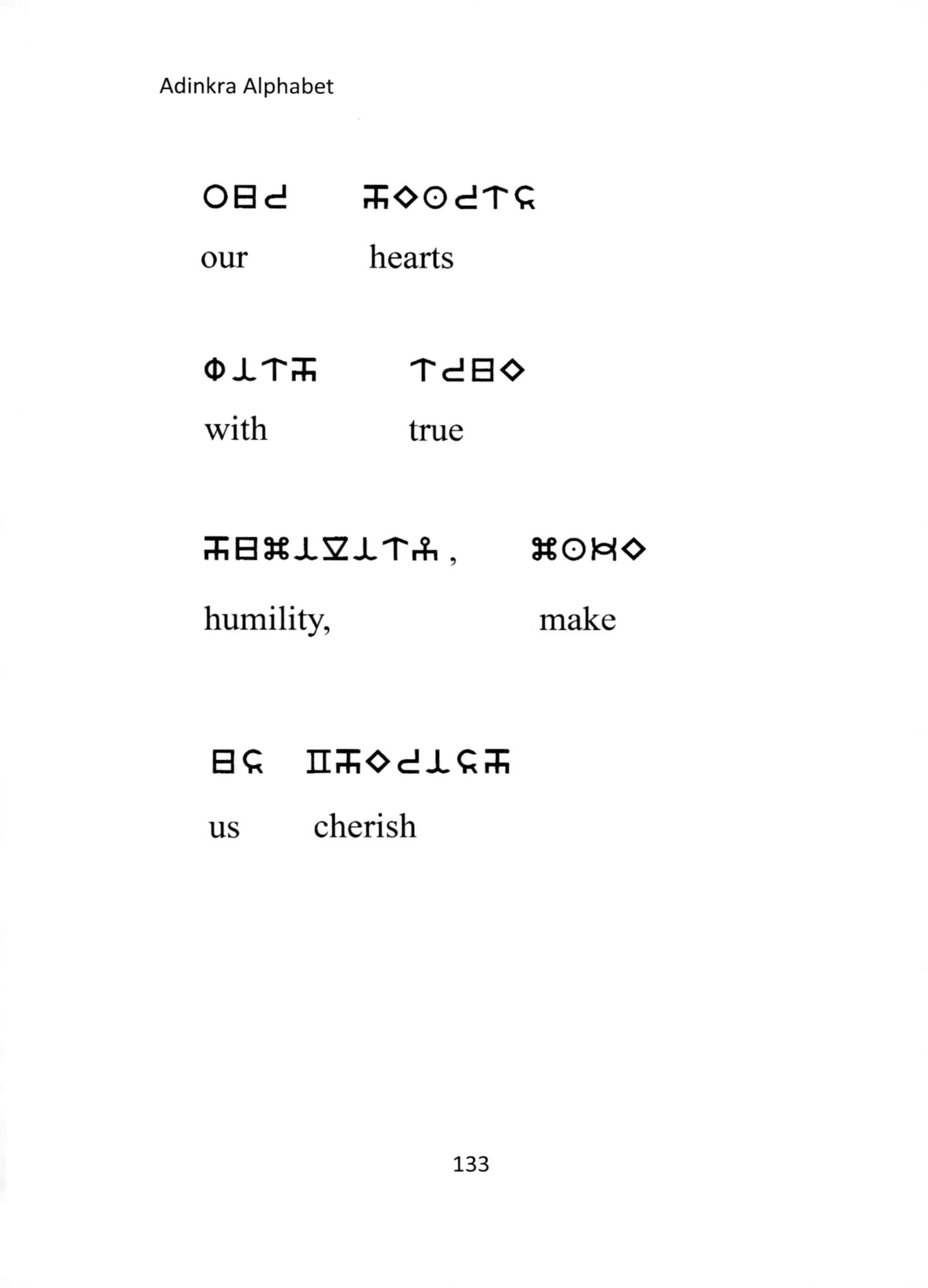

our hearts

with true

humility, make

us cherish

fearless

honesty, and

help us to

resist

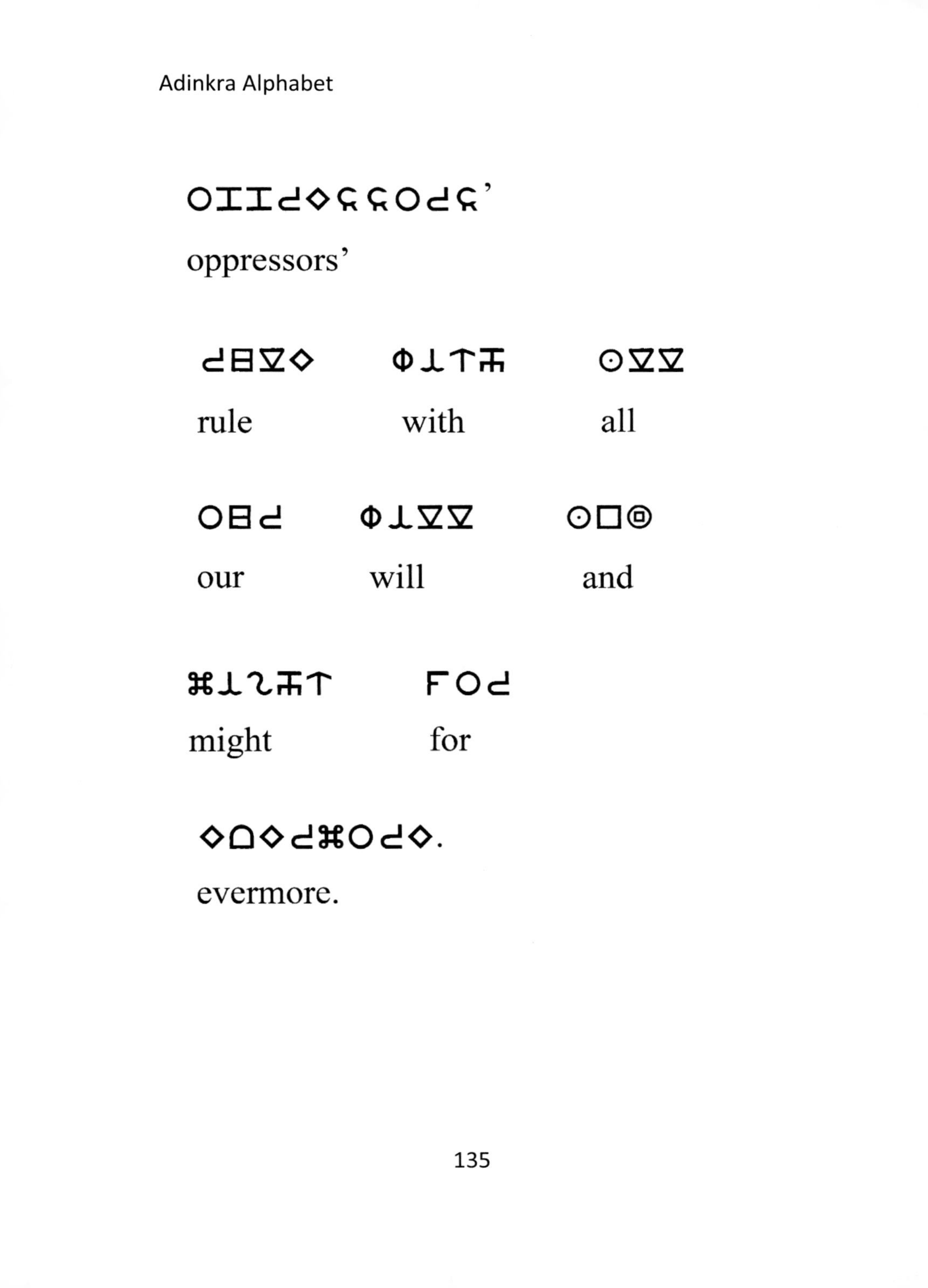

oppressors'

rule with all

our will and

might for

evermore.

Patriotic Song, Akan

yɛn ara asaase ni

yɛn ara asaase ni;
ɛyɛ abɔdenden ma yɛn,
mogya a nananom hwie gui
nya de to hɔ ma yɛn,
edurur me ne wo nso so,
sɛ yɛbɛyɛ bi atoa so,
nimdeɛ ntraso nkotokrane;
ne apɛsɛmenkominya,
edi yɛn bra mu dɛm, ama
yɛn asaase ho dɔ atomu sɛ.

(korɔs 2x)

ɔman no, sɛ ɛbɛyɛ yie o!
ɔman no, sɛ ɛrenyɛ yie o!;
ɛyɛ nsɛnnahɔ sɛ, ɔmanfo bra na ɛkyerɛ.

ɔman no, sɛ ɛbɛ yɛ yie o!
ɔman no sɛ ɛrenyɛ yie o!;
ɛyɛ nsɛnnahɔ sɛ, ɔmanfo bra na ɛkyerɛ.

komposa: dr ephraim amu

Yen Ara Asase Ni

Yɛn ara asaase ni

Ɛyɛ abɔdenden ma yɛn

Mogya a nananom hwie gui, nya de to hɔ ma yɛn,

Edu me ne wo nso so

Sɛ yɛbɛyɛ bi atoa so.

Nimdeɛ ntraso nkotokrane;

Ne apɛsɛmenkomenya,

Edi yɛn bra mu dɛm, ma

Yɛn asaase ho dɔ atomu sɛ.

Korɔs 2x

Ɔman no, sɛ ɛbɛyɛ yie o!,

Ɔman no, sɛ ɛrenyɛ yie o!;

Ɛyɛ nsɛnnahɔ sɛ, ɔmanfo bra na ɛkyerɛ.

Ɔman no, sɛ ɛbɛyɛ yie o!,

Ɔman no, sɛ ɛrenyɛ yie o!;

Ɛyɛ nsɛnnahɔ sɛ, ɔmanfo bra na ɛkyerɛ.

Komposa: Dr. Ephraim Amu.

Ghana National Anthem English

↑卅◇ □⊙↑⊥O□⊙▽ ⊙□↑卅◇⌘

F⊥ᑯϚ↑ Ϛ↑⊙□⌂⊙

ՇO◎ ⅄▽◇ϚϚ O日ᑯ ▽O⌘Ɛ▽⊙□◎ Շ卅⊙□⊙,
⊙□◎ ⌘O⋈◇ O日ᑯ □⊙↑⊥O□ ՇᑯO⊙↑ ⊙□◎
Ϛ↑ᑯO□Շ,
⅄O▽◎ ↑O ◎◇F◇□◎ FOᑯ◇◻◇ᑯ
↑卅◇ ⌶O日Ϛ◇ OF Fᑯ◇◇◎O⌘ ⊙□◎
OF ᑯ⊥Շ卅↑.
F⊥▽▽ O日ᑯ 卅◇⊙ᑯ↑Ϛ ⏀⊥↑卅 ↑ᑯ日◇
卅日⌘⊥▽⊥↑卅
⌘O⋈◇ 日Ϛ ⌶卅◇ᑯ⊥Ϛ卅 F◇⊙ᑯ▽◇ϚϚ
卅O□◇Ϛ↑卅,
⊙□◎ 卅◇▽⌶ 日Ϛ ↑O ᑯ◇Ϛ⊥Ϛ↑ O⌶⌶ᑯ◇ϚϚOᑯϚ'
ᑯ日▽◇
⏀⊥↑卅 ⊙▽▽ O日ᑯ ⏀⊥▽▽ ⊙□◎ ⌘⊥Շ卅↑ FOᑯ
◇◻◇ᑯ⌘Oᑯ◇.

⌶O⌘⌶OϚ◇ᑯ: ⌘ᑯ. ⌶卅⊥▽⊥⌶ ⌶O⌘⊥ Շ卅◇卅O

The National Anthem, English

First Stanza

God bless our homeland Ghana
And make our nation great and strong,
Bold to defend forever
The cause of Freedom and of Right;
Fill our hearts with true humility,
Make us cherish fearless honesty,
And help us to resist oppressors' rule
With all our will and might for evermore.

Composer: Mr. Philip Comi Gheho.

Patriotic Song, Ewe

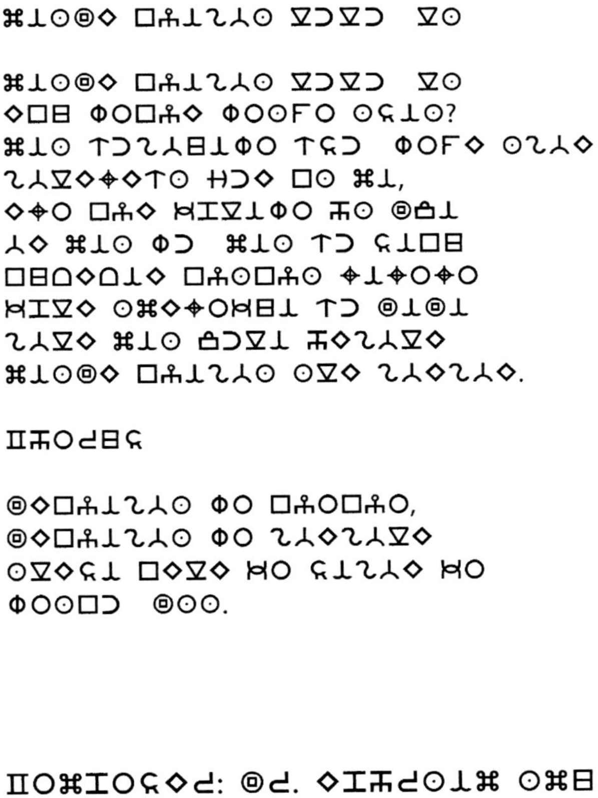

Miade Nyigba Lɔlɔ La

Miade nyigba lɔlɔ la, enu wonye woafo asia?
Mia tɔgbuiwo tsɔ wofe agbe gbleɖeta xɔe na mi,
Eɖo nye kpliwo ha dzi
Be mia wɔ mia tɔ sinu
Nuvevie nyanya, ɖiɖoɖo
Kple ameɖokui tɔ didi
Gble mia zɔli hegble miade nyigba ale gbegbe.

Chorus

Denyigba wo nyonyo, denyigba wo gbegble
Alesi nele ko sigbe ko woanɔ daa.

Composer: Dr. Ephraim Amu

Patriotic Song, Ga

Φ⊃ ◎⊥◇□⊤ʕƐ Φ⊃ ʕ卉⊥⋈IO□ □Ɛ

Φ⊃◎⊥◇□⊤ʕ◇ Φ⊃ ʕ卉⊥⋈IO□ □Ɛ
□⊥ Ɛⵅ' ⅃⊙ Φ⊙ 卉⊙ Φ⊃F◇◇
Φ⊃ ⊤ʕ◇⌘◇⊥ ʕ卉Φ⊥◇ ⊽⊙ ʕ卉⊥
◎⊙□⊥ ⊙⌘◇ ⋈Ɛ 卉◇ 卉⊙ Φ⊃
◇ⵅ⊥ ⌘⊥ ⋈Ɛ ⅄O ᘔ⅄Ɛ□⊙⊙
'⋈Ɛ Φ⊃ 卉⊟ Φ⊃F◇◇ 卉◇ ◇⋈O
ⵅ⊙ □⊥⊽◇◇ ⋈Ɛ 卉◇ʕ⊟⊃⌘⊃ IƐ ⊙⊙⊙□♆◇
Φ⊃ ʕ卉⊥⋈IO□ ⊽◇ ⊙⋈IO
□♆◇ ⅄⊙⊙ □⊥ □♆◇ 卉⊙⊙ Φ⊃⌘⊙□ ⊽◇
卉◇ ʕ⊟O⌘⊃ ⊙卉⊥ Φ⊃ ⌘⊽⊥

Ⅱ卉O⅃⊟ʕ

⋈◇ ⵅ⊥ ⊙⋈ƐƐ ⌘⊙□ ⋈O ⊙⊙⊙卉⊥ ⊽Ɛ
⋈◇ ⵅ⊥ ⊙⋈ƐƐ ⌘⊙□ ⋈O ◇卉⊥⊥ ⊽Ɛ

ⅡO⌘IOʕ◇⅃: ◎⅃ ◇I卉⅃⊙⊥⌘ ⊙⌘⊟

Wɔ Dientsɛ Wɔ Shikpon Nɛ

Wɔdientse wɔ shikpon nɛ
Ni ej' ra wa ha wɔfee
Wɔ tsemei shwie la shi
Dani ame kɛ he ha wɔ
Eji mi kɛ bo gbɛnaa
'Kɛ wɔ hu wɔfee he eko
Ja nilee kɛ hesuɔmɔ pɛ aaanye
Wɔ shikpon le akpo
Nye baa ni nye haa wɔman le
He suomɔ ahi wɔ mli

Chorus
Ke ji akɛɛ man ko aaahi lɛ
Ke ji akɛɛ man ko ehii lɛ

Composer: Dr. Ephraim Amu.

Patriotic Song, Dagbani

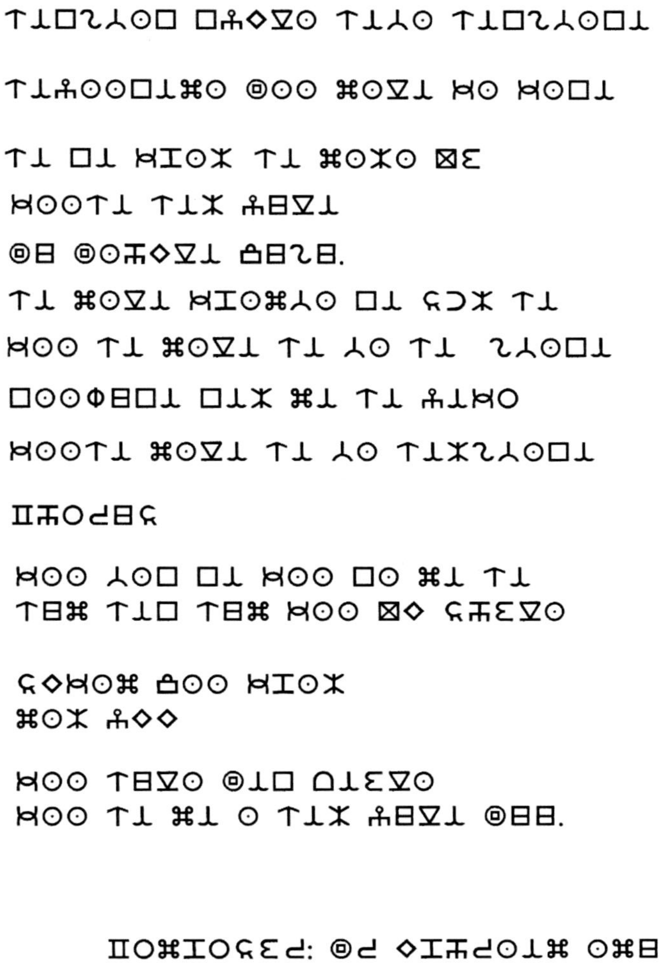

Tingban nyela tiba tingbani

Tiyaanima daa mali ka kani

Ti ni kpaŋ ti maŋa chɛ
Kaati tiŋ yuli
Du dasheli zugu.

Ti mali kpamba ni sɔŋ ti
Kaati mali ti ba tiŋgbani
Naawuni niŋ mi ti yiko
Kaati mali ti ba tiŋgbani

Chorus

Kaa ban ni kaa na mi ti
Tum tin tum kaa che shɛla

Sekam zaa kpaŋ
Maŋ yee

Kaa tula din viɛla
Kaa ti mi a tiŋ yuli duu.

Composer: Dr. Ephraim Amu.

African Countries

---

1. Algeria

2. Angola

3. Benin

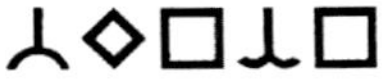

4. Botswana

5. Burkina Faso

6. Burundi

7. Cameroon

8. Cape Verde

9. Central African Republic

10. Chad

11. Comoros

12. Democratic Republic of Congo

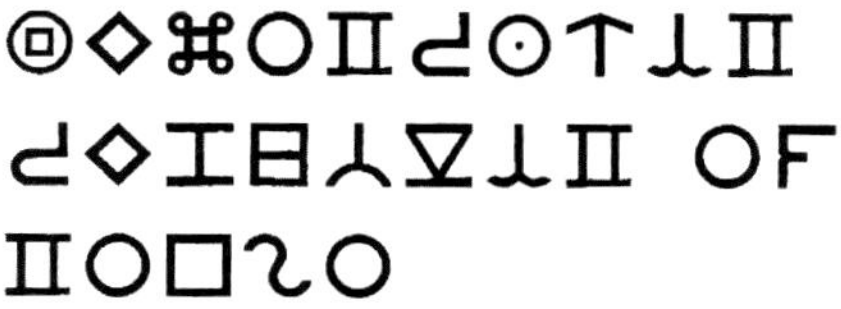

13. Republic of the Congo

14. Djibouti

15. Egypt

16. Equatorial Guinea

17. Eritrea

18. Ethiopia

19. Gabon

20. Gambia

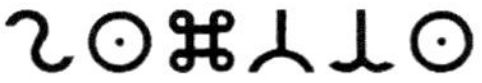

21. Ghana

22. Guinea

23. Guinea-Bissau

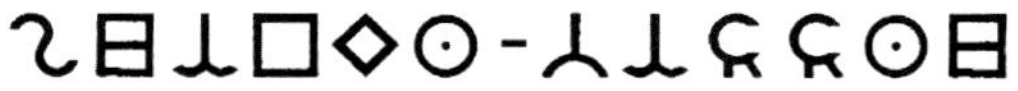

24. Ivory Coast

25. Kenya

26. Lesotho

27. Liberia

28. Libya

29. Madagascar

30. Malawi

31. Mali

32. Mauritania

33. Mauritius

34. Morocco

35. Mozambique

⌘○凸⊙⌘⅄⊥Ψ⊟◇

36. Namibia

□⊙⌘⊥⅄⊥⊙

37. Niger

□⊥ʅ◇ᑯ

38. Nigeria

□⊥ʅ◇ᑯ⊥⊙

39. Rwanda

ᑯΦ⊙□⊡⊙

40. Sao Tome and Principe

⊡⊙○ ↑○⌘◇
⊙□⊡ 工ᑯ⊥□Ⅱ⊥工◇

41. Senegal

ʢ◇□◇ʅ⊙⊻

42. Seychelles

43. Sierra Leone

44. Somalia

45. South Africa

46. South Sudan

47. Sudan

48. Swaziland

49. Tanzania

50. Togo

51. Tunisia

52. Uganda

53. Zambia

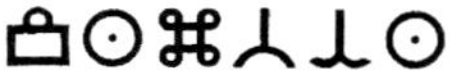

54. Zimbabwe

Numbering System

No.	Adinkra	No.	Adinkra
0	२	13	Ϛ⊙
1	Ϛ	14	Ϛ⊚
2	I	15	ϚO
3	⊙	16	ϚⅡ
4	⊚	17	Ϛ⊟
5	O	18	ϚΨ
6	Ⅱ	19	ϚF
7	⊟	20	I२, ◇
8	Ψ	21	IϚ
9	F	22	II
10	Ϛ२, Ɛ	23	I⊙
11	ϚϚ	24	I⊚
12	ϚI	25	IO

No.	Adinkra	No.	Adinkra
26	IⅡ	39	⊙F
27	I⊟	40	◎ʅ, ⅄
28	IΨ	41	◎Ϛ
29	IF	42	◎I
30	⊙ʅ, ⊥	43	◎⊙
31	⊙Ϛ	44	◎◎
32	⊙I	45	◎○
33	⊙⊙	46	◎Ⅱ
34	⊙◎	47	◎⊟
35	⊙○	48	◎Ψ
36	⊙Ⅱ	49	◎F
37	⊙⊟	50	○ʅ, ㅠ
38	⊙Ψ	51	○Ϛ

No.	Adinkra	No.	Adinkra
52	○工	66	ⅡⅡ
53	○⊙	67	Ⅱ⊟
54	○◎	68	ⅡΨ
55	○○	69	ⅡF
56	○Ⅱ	70	⊟ᒿ, ⋈
57	○⊟	71	⊟ϛ
58	○Ψ	72	⊟工
59	○F	73	⊟⊙
60	Ⅱᒿ, ⵣ	74	⊟◎
61	Ⅱϛ	75	⊟○
62	Ⅱ工	76	⊟Ⅱ
63	Ⅱ⊙	77	⊟⊟
64	Ⅱ◎	78	⊟Ψ
65	Ⅱ○	79	⊟F

No.	Adinkra	No.	Adinkra
80	ΨႲ, ⊽	91	Fና
81	Ψና	92	F工
82	Ψ工	93	F⊙
83	Ψ⊙	94	F◎
84	Ψ◎	95	F○
85	Ψ○	96	FⅡ
86	ΨⅡ	97	F⊟
87	Ψ⊟	98	FΨ
88	ΨΨ	99	FF
89	ΨF	100	ናႲႲ, □
90	FႲ, ⌘	1000	ናႲႲႲ,×

Original Adinkra Symbols

1. Adinkrahene (a, ⊙, 3)

2. Bi Nka Bi (b, ⅄, 40)

3. Ɔwo Foro Adobɛ (c, Ⅱ, 6)

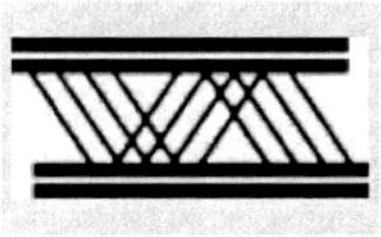

4. Dame-Dame (d, , 4)

5. Ɛban (e, , 20)

6. Fawohodie (f,  , 9)

7. Gye Nyame (g, , 0)

8. Hwemudua (h, , 50)

9. Ɛse Ne Tɛkrɛma (I, , 30)

10.Ɛpa (j, , 60)

11.Kintinkantan (k, , 70)

12.Mmerɛ Dane (l, , 80)

13.Mpatapɔ (m, ⌘, 90)

14.Nkyimu (n, □, 100)

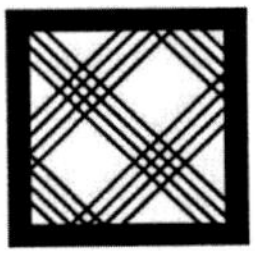

15.Nyame Biribi Wɔ Soro (o, ○, 5)

16.Pempamsie (p, , 2)

17.Denkyɛm (q, , 8)

18.Asase Ye Duru (r, , 200)

19.Sankɔfa (s, , 1)

20.Aya (t, , 300)

21.Nea Onnim No Sua A, Ohu (u, , 7)

22.Bese Saka (v, , 400)

23.Wawa Aba (w, , 500)

24.Akokɔnan (x, , 600)

25.Duafe (y, , 700)

26.Fihankra (z, , 800)

27.Dwennimmɛn (ɛ, , 10)

28.Ɔsram Ne Nsoromma (ɔ, Ↄ, 900)

29.Hye Wonhye (ƒ, ϒ, 1000)

30.Nyame Nnwu Na Mawu (ts, X, 2000)

31.Nyansapɔ (kp,  , 3000)

32.Nsaa (ny,  , 4000)

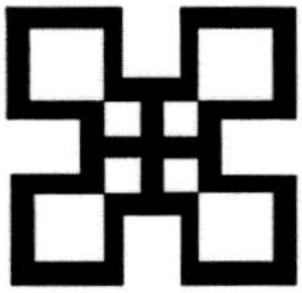

33.Mpuanum (dz,  , 5000)

34.Akoma (ʊ, , 6000)

35.Funtunfunefu-Dɛnkyɛmfunefu

(ɖ, , 7000)

36.Nkɔnsɔnkɔnsɔn (ŋ, , 8000)

37.Ɔkɔdeɛ Mmɔwerɛ (ɣ,  , 9000)

38.Mframadan (ch, , 10,000)

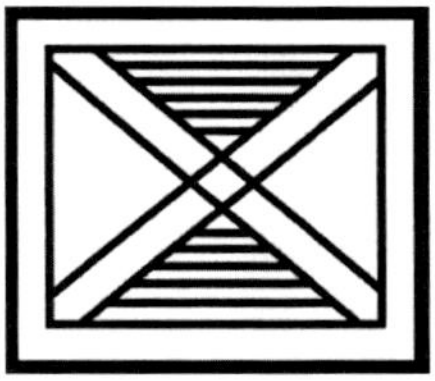

39.Mate Masie (gb, , 11,000)

40.Nkyinkyim (ʒ, ᴨ, 12,000)

41.Kɛtɛ Pa (sh, #, 13,000)

42.Nsoromma (⊙, ⊥, 14,000)

43.Ɔsram (☾, ∪, 15,000)

44.Boa Me Na Me Mmoa Wo (☿, △̄, 16,000)

45.Ɔdɔ Nyera Fie Kwan (♀, ♄, 17,000)

46.Fofo (⊕, , 18,000)

47.1Akobɛn (♂ ,  , 19,000)

47.2Akofena (♂ , , 19,000)

48.1 Kwatakye Atikɔ (♃,  , 20,000)

48.2 Gyawu Atikɔ (♃ ,  , 20,000)

49.Musuyideɛ (♄, ▽, 21,000)

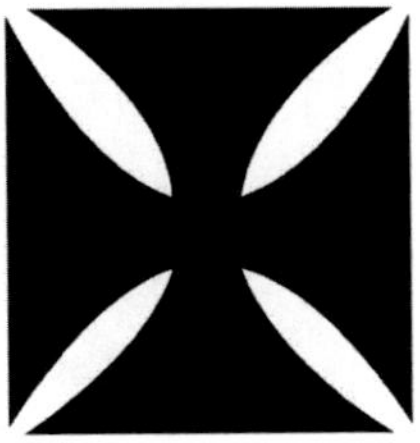

50.Owuo Atwedeɛ (♅, , 22,000)

51.Sunsum (♆, , 23,000)

52.Nyame Dua (☥, , 24,000)

Proverbs, Sayings and Objects associated with Adinkra symbols

1. *Adinkrahene*
   Akan Proverb: "Nea ɔpɛ sɛ obedi hene daakye no firi aseɛ sua som ansa."
   English Transliteration: He/She who wants to become king in the future begins by learning how to serve.
2. *Bi Nka Bi*
   Akan Proverb: "Obi nka obi."
   English Transliteration: Bite not one another.
3. *Ɔwɔ Foro Adobɛ*
   Akan Proverb: "Ɔwɔ foro dobɛ."
   English Transliteration: A snake climbs the raffia palm.
4. *Dame Dame*
   Associated Object – Checkerboard game
5. *Ɛban*
   Associated Object - Fence
6. *Fawohodie*
   Akan Saying: "Fawohodie ene obrɛ na ɛnam."
   English Translation: Independence comes with its responsibilities.
7. *Gye Nyame*
   Akan Proverb: "Abodeɛ santan yi firi tete; obi nte ase a onim n'ahyase, na obi ntena ase nkosi n'awie, gye Nyame."
   English Transliteration: This Great Panorama of creation dates back to time immemorial, no

one lives who saw its beginning and no one will live to see its end, Except God.

8. *Hwemudua*

   Associated Object – Measuring Stick.

9. *Ɛse Ne Tɛkrɛma*

   Akan Proverb: "Wɔnnwo ba ne se."

   English Transliteration: No child is born with teeth.

   English Translation: We improve and advance.

10. *Ɛpa*

    Akan Proverb: "Nea ne pa da wonsa no na woyɛ nakoa."

    English Transliteration: You are the subject of he/she whose handcuffs are around you.

11. *Kintinkantan*

    Akan Saying: "Kin-tin-kan-tan."

    English Transliteration: Puffed up extravagance.

12. *Mmerɛ Dane*

    Akan Saying: "Mmerɛ Dane."

    English Transliteration: Time changes.

13. *Mpatapɔ*

    Akan Saying: "Mpata pɔ."

    English Transliteration: Knot of reconciliation.

14. *Nkyimu*

    Associated Object - Divider

15. *Nyame Biribi Wɔ Soro*

    Akan Proverb: "Nyame biribi wɔ soro na ma me nsa nka!"

English Transliteration: God, there is something in the heavens, pray let it reach me!

16. *Pempamsie*

    Akan Saying: "Pempamsie sɛ bebrebe ahoɔden ne koro yɛ."

    English Translation: Unity is strength

17. *Dɛnkyɛm*

    Akan Proverb: "Dɛnkyɛm da nsuo mu nso ɔhome mframa."

    English Transliteration: The crocodile lives in water yet it breathes air not water.

18. *Asase Ye Duru*

    Akan Proverb: "Asase ye duru sen po."

    English Transliteration: The earth is heavier than the sea.

19. *Sankɔfa*

    Akan Proverb: "Sɛ wo werɛ fi na wo sankɔfa a yenkyi."

    English Transliteration: It is not a taboo to return and fetch it when you forget.

20. *Aya*

    Associated Object – Fern plant (pteridophyte species)

21. *Nea Onnim No Sua A, Ohu*

    Akan Proverb: "Nea onnim no sua a, ohu."

    English Transliteration: He/she who does not know, will know from learning.

22. *Bese Saka*
    Associated Object – Bag of Cola nuts.
23. Wawa Aba

    Twi Saying: "Ɔyɛ den sɛ wawa aba."

    English Transliteration: He is tough as the seed of the wawa tree.

24. *Akokɔnan*
    Akan Proverb: "Akokɔ nan tia ne ba, na enkum no."
    English Transliteration: If a hen treads on her young ones, it does not mean to kill them.
25. *Duafe*
    Associated Object – Wooden comb.
26. *Fihankra*
    Akan Proverb – Yebisa sɛ kyerɛ me osimasi ne fie, nyɛ ne sika dodoɔ a ɔwɔ.
    English Transliteration: We ask to be shown one's house, not how much money one has.
27. *Dwennimmɛn*
    Akan Proverb: "Dwenini yɛ asisie a ɔde nakoma, na ɛnnyɛ ne mmɛn."
    English Transliteration: The ram may bully, not with its horns but with his heart.
28. *Ɔsram Ne Nsoromma*
    Akan Proverb: "Kyɛkyɛ pɛ aware."
    English Transliteration: Kyɛkyɛ (the North Pole Star-Polaris) has a deep love for marriage.

She is always in the sky waiting for the return of the moon, her husband.

29. *Hye Wonhye*

    Akan Saying: "Hye Wonhye."

    English Transliteration: That which cannot be burnt.

30. *Nyame Nwu Na Mawu*

    Akan Saying: "Nyame nwu na mawu."

    English Transliteration: God does not die, and so I cannot die.

31. *Nyansapɔ*

    Akan Proverb: "Nyansapɔ, yɛde Nyansa na ɛsane."

    English Transliteration: It is the wise who unties the wisdom knot.

32. *Nsaa*

    Akan Proverb: "Nea onim nsaa na ɔtɔ nea ago."

    English Transliteration: The one who knows nsaa is willing to buy one even when he knows that it is old.

33. *Mpuanum*

    Associated Object – Traditional five tufts of hair style.

34. Akoma

    Akan Saying: "Nya Akoma."

    English Transliteration: Take heart or be patient.

35. *Funtunfunefu-Dɛnkyɛmfunefu*
    Akan Proverb: "Funtunfunefu dɛnkyɛmfunefu, wɔn afuru bom, nso wɔdidi a na wɔreko efiri sɛ aduane dɛ yɛte no wɔ menetwitwie mu."
    English Transliteration: Funtunfunefu and dɛnkyɛmfunefu (Two conjoined crocodiles) have their stomachs joined together yet when they are eating, they fight because the sweetness of the food is felt as it passes through the throat.
36. *Nkɔnsɔnkɔnsɔn*
    Akan Saying: "Yɛ toatoa mu sɛ nkɔnsɔnkɔnsɔn; nkwamu a, yɛtoa mu, owuo mu a yɛtoa mu; abusua mu nnte da."
    English Translation: We are linked in both life and death; Those who share common blood relations never break-apart.
37. *Ɔkɔdeɛ Mmɔwerɛ*
    Associated Object – Talons of the eagle.
38. *Mframadan*
    Associated Object – Wind-Resistant house.
39. *Mate Masie*
    Akan Saying: "Nyansa bun mu ne, mate masie."
    English Translation: Deep wisdom comes out of listening and keeping what is heard.
40. *Nkyinkyim*
    Akan Proverb: "Ɔbra kwan yɛ nkyinkyim."
    English Transliteration: Life's path is full of ups and downs; twists and turns.

41. *Kɛtɛ Pa*
    Associated Object – A very good bed.
42. Nsoromma
    Twi Saying: "Dabi me nsoromma bepue."
    English Transliteration: One day my star will shine.
43. *Ɔsram*
    Akan Proverb: "Ɔsram mmfiti prɛko ntwa ɔman ho."
    English Transliteration: The moon does not cross the earth hastily.
44. *Boa Me Na Me Mmoa Wo*
    Akan Saying: "Boa me na me mmoa wo."
    English Transliteration: Help me and let me help you.
45. Ɔdɔ Nyera Fie Kwan
    Akan Proverb: "Ɔdɔ Nyera fie kwan."

    English Transliteration: Love lights its own path, it never gets lost on its way home.

46. Fofo
    Twi Proverb: "Sɛ nea fofo pɛ ne sɛ gyinatwi abɔ bidie."
    English Transliteration: What the fofo plant wishes is that the gyinatwi seeds should turn dark.
47. *Akoben*
    Associated Object – War horn.

48. Akofena
    Akan Proverb: "Akofena nkunim kɔ a, wɔbɔ afena hyɛ no safohene."
    English Translation: The retiring great warrior always has a royal sword of rest.
49. Kwatakye Atikɔ
    Associated Object – Hair style of Kwatakye (War captain of old Asante).
50. *Gyawu Atikɔ*
    Associated Object – Shaving style on the back of Gyawu's (sub-chief of Bantama in Kumasi, Ghana) head.
51. *Musuyideɛ (Krapa)*
    Akan Saying: "Krapa te sɛ okra, okyiri fi."
    English Transliteration: Sanctity is like a cat, it abhors filth.
52. Owuo Atwedeɛ
    Twi - Owuo Atwedeɛ ɔbaako mforo
    English Translation – Everybody shall climb the ladder of death.
53. *Sunsum*
    Associated Object – The Soul.
54. *Nyame Dua*
    Associated Object – An altar of God.

Phonetics

The pronunciation system is based on the International Phonetic Alphabet system. The IPA is designed to represent the qualities of speech that are part of oral language such as phones, phonemes, intonation and the separation of words and syllables.

Vowels are sounds produced with no constriction in the vocal tract.

Consonants are sounds produced with constriction or closure at some point along the vocal tract.

IPA symbols are composed of letters and diacritics. Diacritics gives the precise sounding of words as they are pronounced. For example, the letters p and t can be represented as [p] and [t] or more precisely as [p^h] and [t^h].

There are no capital letters in the Adinkra alphabet system. The first letter in a word can be distinguished by being written bigger, underlined, dotted or artistically designed as needed to differentiate it from the alphabets following it. When writing with simplified Adinkra alphabet characters, the first letter in a word can be written with standard Adinkra alphabet character if desired.

Vowels originate from the tongue as shown below. Consonants originate from 5 regions as the lips, the teeth, the tongue, the palate and the throat.

Each of these five main regions can be divided into two sub regions to make 10 regions of sound production. The ten regions of sound production correlate with the ten symbols or Sephirots of the Tree of Life. This similarity is what links sound production to creation.

The tongue region is divided into front and back for vowel production. For consonants, the lips are divided into bilabial (bi-two, labial-lips) and labiodental (labio-lips, dental-teeth). The teeth region is divided into dental (teeth) and Alveolar (tooth sockets). The tongue region is divided into post-alveolar (post-behind, alveolar-tooth socket) and Retroflex (retro-backward imitation, flex-bend). The palate into palatal (hard palate) and velar/uvular (soft palate) and the throat into pharyngeal (behind the tongue) and glottal (throat proper).

The flow of air during sound production is also divided into ten different types: two vowels and eight consonants. The airway is either closed or open during vowel production. In general, the airway is fully open during vowel production. There is constriction during consonant production and the turbulence produced is used to classify the different types of air flow during consonant sounds.

Stop or plosive consonants are produced when the airflow is completely blocked in both the airway and nasal passages. When there is flow through the nose in stop consonants the sound is nasal. Fricative consonants are produced when there is partial blockage and therefore strongly turbulent airflow in the airway. Lateral fricatives are a type of fricative where the frication occurs on one or both sides of the edge of the tongue.

Approximants are produced when there is minimal blockage of the airway with only slight turbulence. Lateral approximant are a type of approximant produced with the side of the tongue.

When the airstream causes the articulator (the tongue) to vibrate a thrill is produced and a Tap/Flap is produced when there is momentary closure of the oral cavity.

Correspondence between Airflow in sound, The Adinkra Tree of Life and the Kabbalistic Tree of Life

Tap sound where the tip of the tongue touches the roof of the mouth forms the crown.

Tongue stays low and is vibrated by the airstream in Thrill and this form the Kingdom. The front and back vowels form the middle pathway beauty and foundation respectively.

Plosive, fricative and lateral fricative form the right column whiles nasal, approximate and lateral approximate form the left column.

Sound	Adinkra Tree of life correspondence	Kabbalistic Tree of Life correspondence
Tap	Gye Nyame	Crown
Nasal	Sankɔfa	Wisdom
Plosive	Pempamsie	Understanding
Fricative	Dame-Dame	Severity
Approximate	Adinkrahene	Mercy
Front Vowel	Nyame Biribi Wɔ Soro	Beauty
Lateral Fricative	Nea Onnim No Sua A, Ohu	Splendor
Lateral Approximate	Ɔwo Foro Adobɛ	Victory
Back vowel	Denkyɛm	Foundation
Thrill	Fawohodie	Kingdom

Adinkra Vowels and their Sound

Number	Adinkra Vowel	English/Akan Vowel	Sound
1	⊙	A	a
2	◇	E	i, e
3	⊥	I	I
4	O	O	o, ü,
5	⊟	U	u
6	Ɛ	Ɛ	ɛ
7	⊃	Ɔ	ɔ

Adinkra Consonants and their Sound

Number	Adinkra Consonant	English Consonant	Sound
1		B	b
2		C	c
3		D	d, dw, dwi
4		F	f
5		G	g, gw, gyi
6		H	h, hw, hwi, hyi
7		J	j
8		K	k, kw, kyi,
9		L	l
10		M	m

Number	Adinkra Consonant	English Consonant	Sound
11		N	n, ng, ngi, nw, nwi, nyi/nnyi
12		P	p
13		Q	q
14		R	r
15		S	s
16		T	t, ti, twi
17		V	v
18		W	w, wi
19		X	x
20		Y	y
21		Z	z

ADINKRA ALPHABET

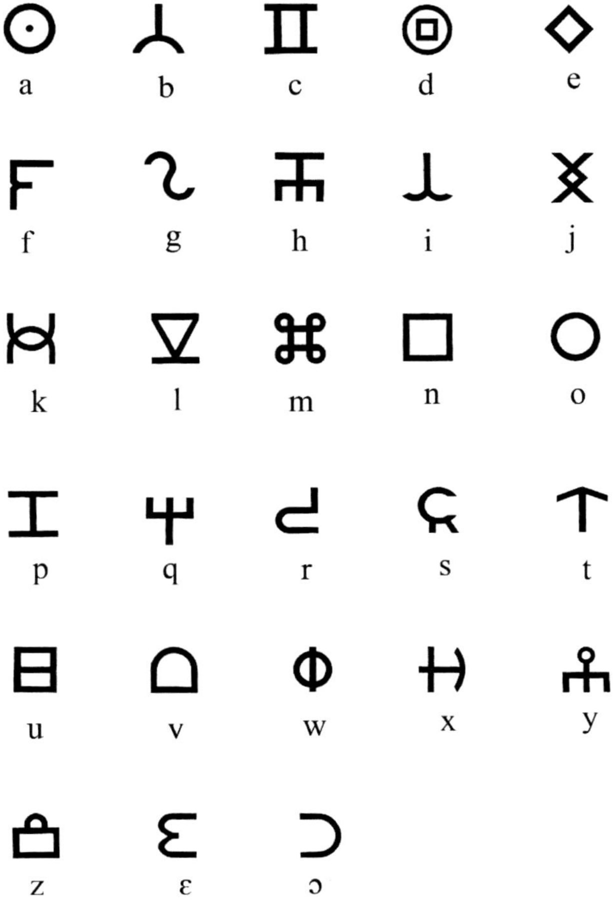
a b c d e
f g h i j
k l m n o
p q r s t
u v w x y
z ɛ ɔ

Akan Table of Vowels

Number	Adinkra Vowel	English/Akan Vowel	Sound
1		A	a
2		E	i, e
3		I	I
4		O	o, ü,
5		U	u
6		Ɛ	ɛ
7		Ɔ	ɔ

Akan Table of Consonants

Number	Adinkra Consonant	English Consonant	Sound
1		B	b
2		D	d, dw, dwi
3		F	f
4		G	g, gw, gyi
5		H	h, hw, hwi, hyi
6		K	k, kw, kyi,
7		L	l
8		M	m

Akan Table of Consonants – Cont.

Number	Adinkra Consonant	English Consonant	Sound
9		N	n, ng, ngi, nw, nwi, nyi/nnyi
10		P	p
11		R	r
12		S	s
13		T	t, ti, twi
14		W	w, wi
15		Y	y
16		Z	z

ADINKRA ALPHABET, AKAN

a b d e ɛ
f g h i k
l m n o ɔ
p r s t u
w y z

Ewe Table of Vowels

Number	Adinkra Vowel	English/Akan Vowel	Sound
1	⊙	A	a
2	◇	E	i, e
3	⊥	I	I
4	○	O	o, ü,
5	⊟	U	u
6	Ɛ	Ɛ	ɛ
7	⊃	Ɔ	ɔ

Ewe Table of Consonants

Number	Adinkra Consonant	English Consonant	Sound
1		B	b
2		C	c
3		D	d, dw, dwi
4		F	f
5		G	g, gw, gyi
6		H	h, hw, hwi, hyi
7		J	j
8		K	k, kw, kyi,
9		L	l
10		M	m

Ewe Table of Consonants – Cont.

Number	Adinkra Consonant	English Consonant	Sound
11		N	n, ng, ngi, nw, nwi, nyi/nnyi
12		P	p
13		Q	q
14		R	r
15		S	s
16		T	t, ti, twi
17		V	v
18		W	w, wi
19		X	x
20		Y	y
21		Z	z

ADINKRA ALPHABET, EWE

a
b
d
ɖ
dz
e
ɛ
f
ƒ
g
gb
ɣ
h
i
k
kp
l
m
n
ny
ŋ
o
ɔ
p
r
s
t
ts
u
v
ʋ
w
x
y
z

Ga (Dangbe) Table of Vowels

Number	Adinkra Vowel	English/Akan Vowel	Sound
1	⊙	A	a
2	◇	E	i, e
3	⊥	I	I
4	O	O	o, ü,
5	⊟	U	u
6	ɛ	Ɛ	ɛ
7	ɔ	Ɔ	ɔ

Ga (Dangbe) Table of Consonants

Number	Adinkra Consonant	English Consonant	Sound
1		B	b
2		C	c
3		D	d, dw, dwi
4		F	f
5		G	g, gw, gyi
6		H	h, hw, hwi, hyi
7		J	j
8		K	k, kw, kyi,
9		L	l
10		M	m

Ga (Dangbe) Table of Consonant – Cont.

Number	Adinkra Consonant	English Consonant	Sound
11		N	n, ng, ngi, nw, nwi, nyi/nnyi
12		P	p
13		Q	q
14		R	r
15		S	s
16		T	t, ti, twi
17		V	v
18		W	w, wi
19		X	x
20		Y	y
21		Z	z

ADINKRA ALPHABET, GA

a b d e ɛ
f g h i j
k l m n ŋ
o ɔ p r s
t u v w y
z

Dagbani Table of Vowels

Number	Adinkra Vowel	English/Akan Vowel	Sound
1	⊙	A	a
2	◇	E	i, e
3	⊥	I	I
4	O	O	o, ü,
5	⊟	U	u
6	Ɛ	Ɛ	ɛ
7	Ɔ	Ɔ	ɔ

Dagbani Table of Consonants

Number	Adinkra Consonant	English Consonant	Sound
1		B	b
2		C	c
3		D	d, dw, dwi
4		F	f
5		G	g, gw, gyi
6		H	h, hw, hwi, hyi
7		J	j
8		K	k, kw, kyi,
9		L	l
10		M	m

Dagbani Table of Consonants – Cont.

Number	Adinkra Consonant	English Consonant	Sound
11		N	n, ng, ngi, nw, nwi, nyi/nnyi
12		P	p
13		Q	q
14		R	r
15		S	s
16		T	t, ti, twi
17		V	v
18		W	w, wi
19		X	x
20		Y	y
21		Z	z

ADINKRA ALPHABET, DAGBANI

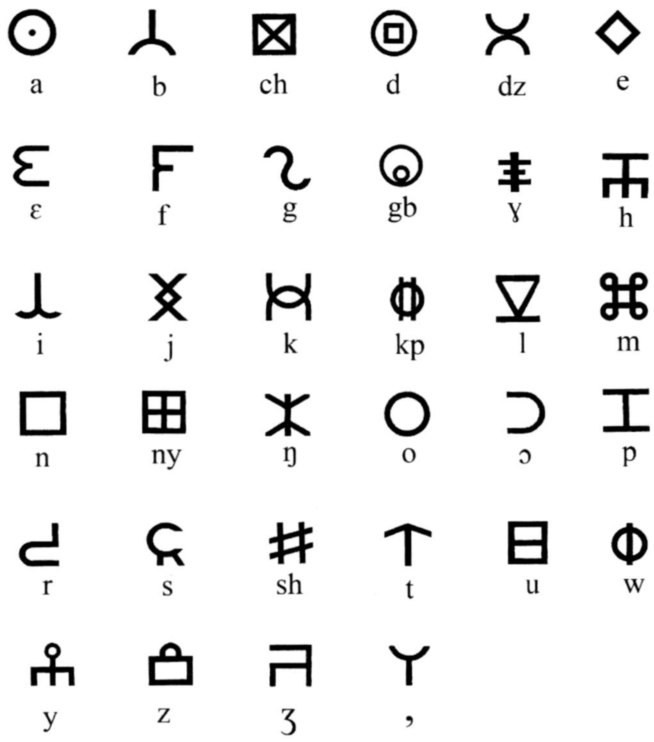
a b ch d dz e
ɛ f g gb ɣ h
i j k kp l m
n ny ŋ o ɔ p
r s sh t u w
y z ʒ ’

Adinkra Alphabet Details of Sound Productions

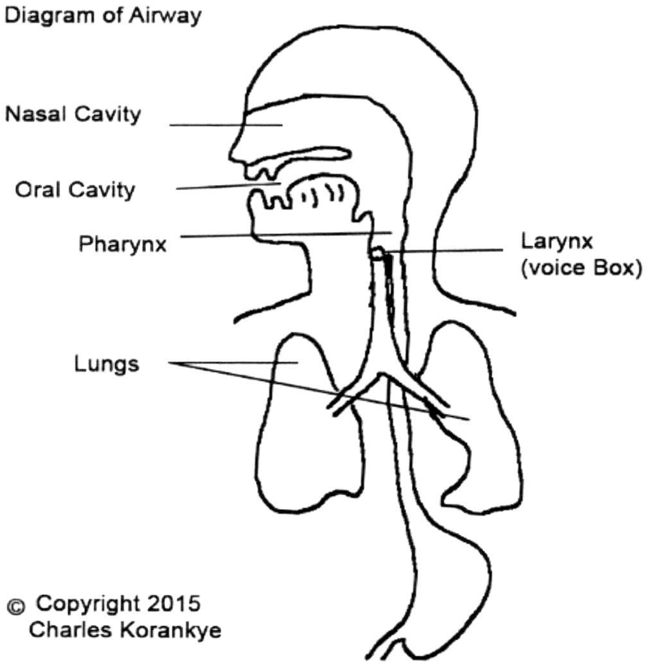
Diagram of Airway
Nasal Cavity
Oral Cavity
Pharynx
Larynx
(voice Box)
Lungs
© Copyright 2015
Charles Korankye

Detailed Diagram of Airway

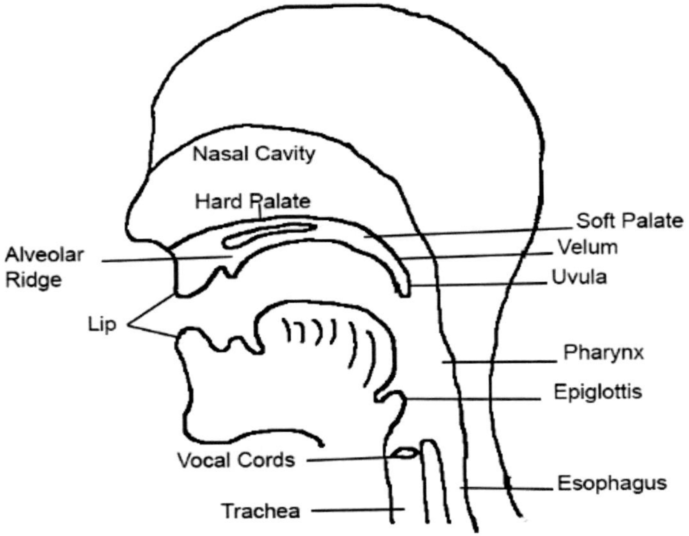
Nasal Cavity
Hard Palate
Soft Palate
Velum
Alveolar Ridge
Uvula
Lip
Pharynx
Epiglottis
Vocal Cords
Esophagus
Trachea

Adinkra Alphabet Phonetic Vowels Diagram

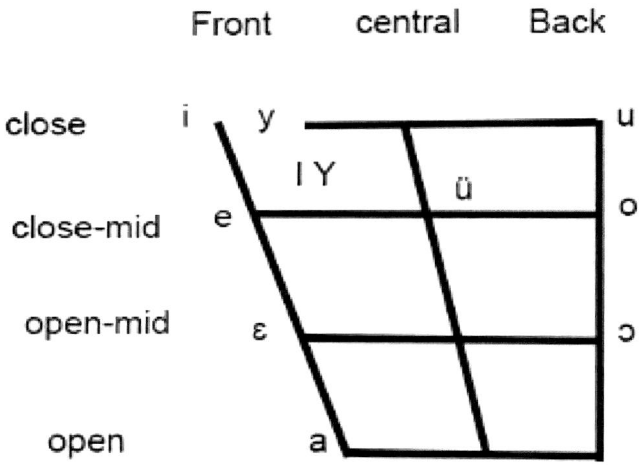
Front
central
Back
close
i
y
u
I Y
ü
close-mid
e
o
open-mid
ɛ
ɔ
open
a

Tongue Position of Vowels

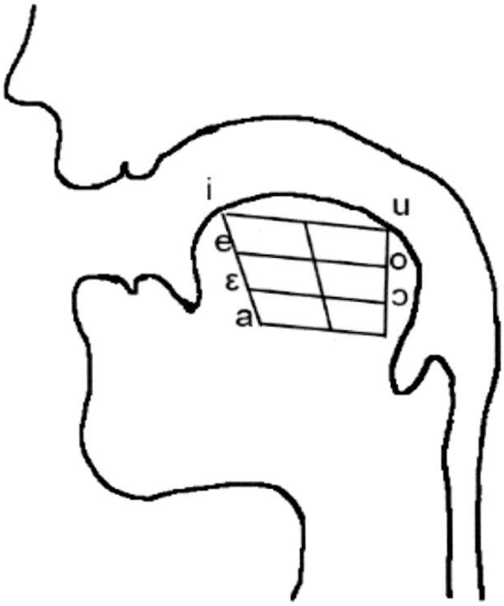
i
u
e
o
ɛ
ɔ
a

International Phonetic Alphabet (IPA) Vowels chart

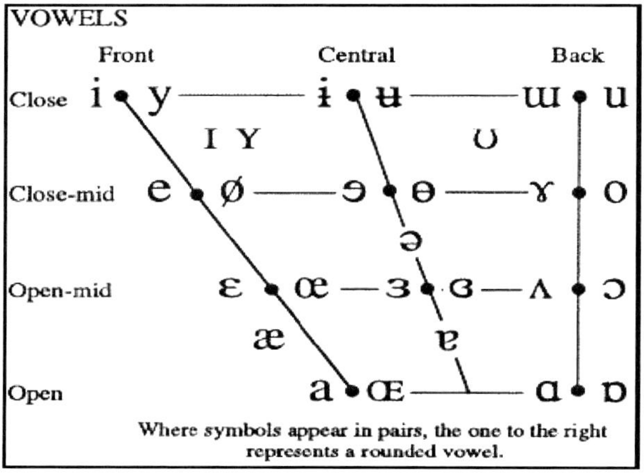
VOWELS
Front
Central
Back
Close
Close-mid
Open-mid
Open
i y ɨ ʉ ɯ u
ɪ ʏ ʊ
e ø ɘ ɵ ɤ o
ə
ɛ œ ɜ ɞ ʌ ɔ
æ ɐ
a ɶ ɑ ɒ
Where symbols appear in pairs, the one to the right represents a rounded vowel.

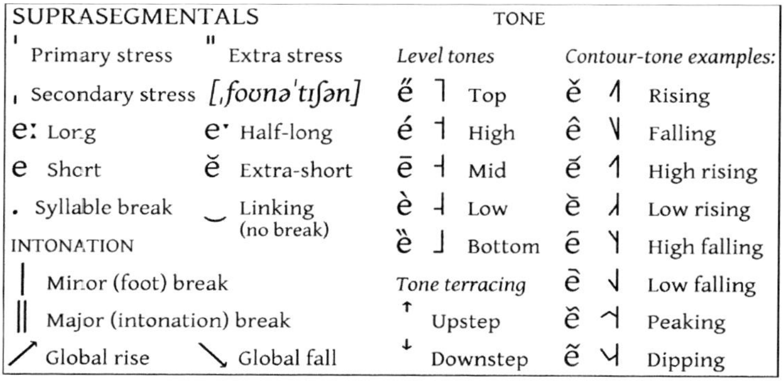
SUPRASEGMENTALS
ˈ Primary stress
ˈˈ Extra stress
ˌ Secondary stress
[ˌfoʊnəˈtɪʃən]
eː Long
eˑ Half-long
e Short
ĕ Extra-short
. Syllable break
‿ Linking (no break)
INTONATION
| Minor (foot) break
‖ Major (intonation) break
↗ Global rise
↘ Global fall
TONE
Level tones
e̋ ˥ Top
é ˦ High
ē ˧ Mid
è ˨ Low
ȅ ˩ Bottom
Tone terracing
ꜛ Upstep
ꜜ Downstep
Contour-tone examples:
ě Rising
ê Falling
e᷄ High rising
e᷅ Low rising
e᷇ High falling
e᷆ Low falling
e᷈ Peaking
e᷉ Dipping

(Source: www.internationalphoneticalphabet.org)

Adinkra Alphabet Phonetic, Consonants Chart-Lips, Teeth and Tongue

	Bilabial	Labio-dental	Dental	Alveolar	Post-alveolar	Retroflex
Plosive	**p b**			**t d**		
Nasal	**m**			**n**		
Trill	**B**			**r**		
Tap or flap				**ɾ**		**ɽ**
Fricative		**f v**		**S Z**	**3**	
Lateral fricative						
Approximant						
Lateral approximant						

Adinkra Alphabet Phonetic, Consonants Chart-Palate and Throat

	Palatal	Velar	Uvular	Pharyngeal	Glottal
Plosive	**c**	**k g**	**q G**		
Nasal	**ɲ**	**ŋ**	**N**		
Trill or flap			**R**		
Fricative	**ç**	**X**			**h**
Lateral fricative					
Approximant	**j**	**ɰ**			
Lateral approximant					

Airway Position of Consonants

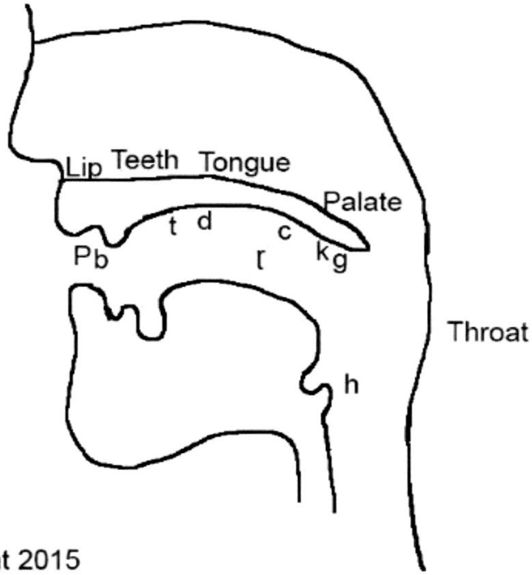
Lip
Teeth
Tongue
Palate
t d
c
Pb
ɾ
kg
Throat
h

Akan Pronunciation-Vowels

Akan Vowel	Vowel	Pronunciation
⊙	**a**	[a]
⊙	**a**	[æ]
⊙	**a**	[ao]
◇	**e**	[e]
◇	**e**	[eɛ]
◇	**e**	[ei]
	**i**	[i]
	**i**	[ia]
	**i**	[ie]

Akan Pronunciation - Vowels Cont.

Akan Vowel	Vowel	Pronunciation
⊥	**i**	[ii] or [i:]
O	**o**	[o]
O	**o**	[ʊ]
O	**o**	[o:] or [oo]
O	**o**	[oɔ]
⊃	**ɔ**	[ɔ]
⊟	**u**	[u]
⊟	**u**	[ue]
⊟	**u**	[uo]
ɛ	**ɛ**	[ɛ]

Akan Pronunciation Vowels Simplified

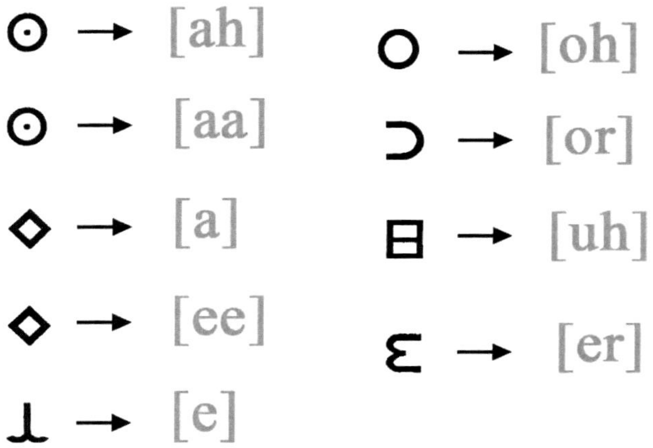
[ah]
[aa]
[a]
[ee]
[e]
[oh]
[or]
[uh]
[er]

[a] – Short "a"

[aa] – Long "a"

[e] – Short "e"

[ee] – Long "e"

Akan Pronunciation - Consonants

Akan Consonant	Consonant	Pronunciation
	**b**	[b]
	**d**	[d]
	**dw**	[dʒ]
	**dwi**	[dʑ^{w}i ~ji]
	**f**	[f]
	**g**	[g]
	**gw**	[g^{w}]
	**gyi**	[dʑi]
	**h**	[h]
	**hw**	[h^{w}]

Akan Pronunciation Consonants Cont.

Akan Consonant	Consonant	Pronunciation
	**hwi**	[ç^{w}i]
	**hyi**	[çi]
	**k**	[k^{h}]
	**kw**	[k^{w}]
	**kyi**	[tɕ^{h}i~cç^{h}i]
	**l**	[l]
	**m**	[m]
	**n**	[n, ŋ, ɲ]
	**ng**	[ŋ:]
	**ngi**	[ɲi]

Akan Pronunciation Consonants Cont.

Akan Consonant	Consonant	Pronunciation
	**nw**	[ŋŋ^{w}]
	**nwi**	[ɲ^{w}i]
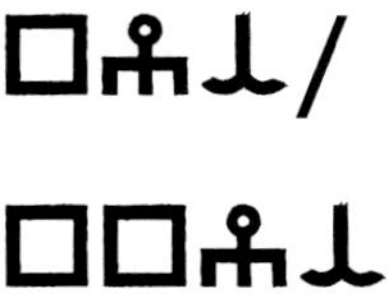	**nyi/nnyi**	[ɲ:i]
	**p**	[p^{h}]
	**r**	[ɾ, r, ɽ]
	**s**	[s]
	**t**	[t^{h}]
	**ti**	[tçi]

Akan Pronunciation Consonants Cont.

Akan Consonant	Consonant	Pronunciation
	**twi**	[tɕ^{w}i]
	**w**	[w]
	**wi**	[ɰi]
	**y**	[y]
	**z**	[z]

Akan Diacritics

t^w d^w Labialized

Ü centralized

Akan Co-articulated

M W Voiceless/Voiced labial-Velar approximants

ɕ ʑ Voiceless/voiced alveolo-palatal fricatives

t͜s, k͡p, Double articulations are represented by two symbols joined by a tie bar.

Adinkra Alphabet Akan Phonetic Vowel Position Table

Orthographic	+ATR	-ATR
i	i, ia, ie, i:	
e	e,	i, ei
ɛ		ɛ
a	æ	a, ao
ɔ		ɔ
o	o, oɔ	ʊ, o:,
u	u, ue, uo	

+ATR = Advanced tongue root or tense vowels

-ATR = Retracted tongue root or lax vowels

Adinkra Alphabet Akan Phonetic, Consonants Chart-Lips, Teeth and Tongue

	Bilabial	Labio-dental	Dental	Alveolar	Post-alveolar	Retroflex
Plosive	**P b**			**t d**		
Nasal	**m**			**n ngi** **ng** **nyi**		
Trill				**r**		
Tap or flap						
Fricative		**f v**		**S**		
Lateral fricative						
Approximant						
Lateral approximant						

Adinkra Alphabet Akan Phonetic, Consonants Chart-Palate and Throat

	Palatal	Velar	Uvular	Pharyngeal	Glottal
Plosive	tɕ^{h}i~cç^{h}i dʒ	**k g**	**kw gw**		
Nasal	**ɲ**	**ŋ**	**N**		
Trill or flap			**R**		
Fricative	**çi h**				
Lateral fricative					
Approximant		**ɰ**			
Lateral approximant					

Ewe Pronunciation-Vowels

Ewe Vowel	Vowel	Pronunciation
	**a**	[a]
	**a**	[ã]
	**e**	[e]
	**e**	[ẽ]
	**i**	[i]
	**i**	[ĩ]
	**o**	[o]
	**o**	[õ]

Ewe Vowel Pronunciation – Cont.

Ewe Vowel	Vowel	Pronunciation
	u	[u]
	u	[ũ]
	ε	[ε]
	ε	[ε̃]
	ɔ	[ɔ]
	ɔ	[ɔ̃]

The tilde (~) marks nasal vowels.

Ewe Pronunciation - Consonants

Ewe Consonant	Consonant	Pronunciation
	**b**	[b]
	**d**	[d]
	**dy**	[ɖ]
	ɖ	[ɖ]
	**dz**	[dz]
	**dzi**	[dʒi]
	**f**	[f]
	ƒ	[ɸ]
	**g**	[g]
	**gb**	[gb]
	ɣ	[ɣ~ʁ]
	**h**	[h]

Ewe Consonant Pronunciation – Cont.

Ewe Consonant	Consonant	Pronunciation
	**k**	[k]
	**kp**	**[k͡p]**
	**l**	[l]
	**m**	[m/m]
	**n**	[n]
	**ny**	[ɲ]
	ŋ	[ŋ]
	ŋw	
	**p**	[p]
	**r**	[r]
	**s**	[s]
	**si**	[ʃi]

Ewe Consonant Pronunciation – Cont.

Ewe Consonant	Consonant	Pronunciation
	**t**	[t]
	**ty**	[ţ]
	**ts**	[ts]
	tsi	[ʧi]
	**v**	[v]
	ʋ	[ʋ]
	**w**	[w]
	**x**	[x]
	**y**	[y]
	**z**	[z]
	**zi**	[ʒi]

Adinkra Alphabet Ewe Phonetic Vowel Position Table

	Front	Back
Close	i, ĩ	u, ũ
Close-mid	e, ẽ	o, õ
Open-mid	ɛ, ɛ̃	ɔ, ɔ̃
Open	a, ã	

Adinkra Alphabet Ewe Phonetic, Consonants Chart-Lips, Teeth and Tongue

	Bilabial	Labio-dental	Dental	Alveolar	Post-alveolar	Retroflex
Plosive	**p** **m**~b			**t d**		**n**~ ɖ
Nasal						
Trill						
Tap or flap						
Fricative	ɸ β	**f v**		**S Z**		
Lateral fricative				**l**~ ĩ		
Approximant						
Lateral approximant						

Adinkra Alphabet Ewe Phonetic, Consonants Chart-Palate and Throat

	Palatal	Velar	Uvular	Pharyngeal	Glottal
Plosive	**ɲ~j**	**k** **ŋ~g**		k͡p g͡b	
Nasal					
Trill or flap					
Fricative		x ɣ~w			ʁ/ɦ
Lateral fricative					
Approximant					
Lateral approximant					

Affricate Voiceless : t͡s

Affricate Voiced: d͡z

Ga Pronunciation-Vowels

Ga Vowel	Vowel	Pronunciation
⊙	**a**	[a]
⊙	**a**	[ã]
◇	**e**	[e]
◇	ẽ	[ẽ]
ɛ	**ɛ**	[ɛ]
ɛ	ɛ̃	[ɛ̃]
⊥	**i**	[i]
⊥	ĩ	[ĩ]

Ga Vowel Pronunciation – Cont.

Ga Vowel	Vowel	Pronunciation
	**o**	[o]
	õ	[õ]
	**ɔ**	[ɔ]
	ɔ̃	[ɔ̃]
	**u**	[u]
	ũ	[ũ]

Ga Pronunciation - Consonants

Ga Consonant	Consonant	Pronunciation
	**b**	[b]
	**d**	[d]
	**f**	[f]
	**g**	[g]
	**gb**	[gb]
	**gw**	[g^{w}]
	**h**	[h]
	**hw**	[h^{w}]
	**j**	[ʤ]
	**jw**	[ʤ^{w}]
	**k**	[k]

Ga Pronunciation Consonants – Cont.

Ga Consonant	Consonant	Pronunciation
	**kp**	[kp]
	**kw**	[k^w]
	**l**	[l]
	**m**	[m]
	**n**	[n]
	**ny**	[ɲ]
	ŋ	[ŋ]
	ŋm	[ŋm]
	ŋw	[$ŋ^w$]
	**p**	[p]
	**r**	[r]

Ga Pronunciation Consonants – Cont.

Ga Consonant	Consonant	Pronunciation
	**s**	[s]
	**sh**	[ʃ]
	**shw**	[ʃʷ]
	**t**	[t]
	**ts**	[tʃ]
	**tsw**	[tʃʷ]
	**v**	[v]
	**w**	[w]
	**y**	[j]
	**z**	[z]

Adinkra Alphabet Ga Phonetic Vowel Position Table

	Front		Central		Back	
	oral	nasal	oral	nasal	oral	nasal
Close	i	ĩ			u	ũ
Close-mid	e	ẽ			o	
Open-mid	ɛ	ɛ̃			ɔ	ɔ̃
Open			a	ã		

Adinkra Alphabet Ga Phonetic-Consonants Chart-Lips, Teeth and Tongue

	Bilabial	Labio-dental	Dental	Alveolar	Post-alveolar	Retroflex
Plosive	**p** b			**t d**	tʃ ʤ tʃʷ ʤʷ	
Nasal	**m**		**n**		ɲ	
Trill						
Tap or flap						
Fricative		**f v**		**S Z**	ʃ ʃʷ	
Lateral fricative						
Approximant			**l**		**j** ɥ	
Lateral approximant						

Adinkra Alphabet Ga Phonetic-consonants Chart-Palate and Throat

	Palatal	Velar	Uvular	Pharyngeal	Glottal
Plosive		**k g** **k^w g^w**		$\widehat{kp}$ $\widehat{gb}$	
Nasal		**ŋ**		$\widehat{ŋm}$	
Trill or flap					
Fricative					h h^w
Lateral fricative					
Approximant		w			
Lateral approximant					

Dagbani Pronunciation-Vowels

Dagbani Vowel	Vowel	Pronunciation
	**a**	[a]
	**a:**	[a:]
	**e**	[e]
	e:	[e:]
	**i**	[i]
	i:	[i:]
	**i**	[i]

Dagbani Vowel Pronunciation – Cont.

Dagbani Vowel	Vowel	Pronunciation
O	**o**	[o]
O	o:	[o:]
⊟	**u**	[u]
⊟	**u:**	[u:]
Ɛ	**ɛ**	[ɛ]

Dagbani Pronunciation - Consonants

Dagbani Consonant	Consonant	Pronunciation
	**b**	[b]
	**ch**	[tʃ]
	**d**	[d]
	dz	[dz]
	**f**	[f]
	**g**	[g]
	**gb**	[gb]
	ɣ	[ɣ]
	**h**	[h]
	**j**	[j]
	k	[k]

Dagbani Consonant Pronunciation – Cont.

Dagbani Consonant	Consonant	Pronunciation
	**kp**	**[k͡p]**
	**l**	[l]
	**m**	[m]
	**n**	[n]
	**ny**	[ɲ]
	ŋ	[ŋ]
	ŋm	[ŋ͡m]
	p	[p]
	**r**	[r]
	**s**	[s]

Dagbani Consonant Pronunciation – Cont.

Dagbani Consonant	Consonant	Pronunciation
	**sh**	[ʃ]
	**t**	[t]
	**v**	[v]
	w	[w]
	**v**	[ʊ]
	y	[j]
	**z**	[z]
	**x**	[x]
	**ʒ**	[ʒ]

Adinkra Alphabet Dagbani Phonetic Vowel Position Table

Short Vowels

	Front	Central	Back
High	i		u
Mid	e		o
Low		a	

Long Vowels

	Front	Central	Back
High	i:		u:
Mid	e:		o:
Low		a:	

aa - [a:]

ii – [i:]

uu – [u:]

Adinkra Alphabet Dagbani Phonetic-Consonants Chart-Lips, Teeth and Tongue

	Bilabial	Labio-dental	Dental	Alveolar	Post-alveolar	Retroflex
Plosive	**p** b			**t d**		
Nasal	**m**			**n**		
Trill						
Tap or flap						
Fricative		**f v**		**S Z**		
Lateral fricative				**l**		
Approximant		ʋ		**r**		
Lateral approximant						

Adinkra Alphabet Dagbani Phonetic-consonants Chart-Palate and Throat

	Palatal	Velar	Uvular	Pharyngeal	Glottal
Plosive		**k g**		k͡p g͡b	
Nasal	ɲ	ŋ		ŋ͡m	
Trill or flap					
Fricative					
Lateral fricative					
Approximant	**j**				
Lateral approximant					

International Phonetic Alphabet Consonants Chart

CONSONANTS (PULMONIC)

	Bilabial	Labiodental	Dental	Alveolar	Postalveolar	Retroflex	Palatal	Velar	Uvular	Pharyngeal	Glottal
Plosive	p b			t d		ʈ ɖ	c ɟ	k g	q ɢ		ʔ
Nasal	m	ɱ		n		ɳ	ɲ	ŋ	ɴ		
Trill	ʙ			r					ʀ		
Tap or Flap				ɾ		ɽ					
Fricative	ɸ β	f v	θ ð	s z	ʃ ʒ	ʂ ʐ	ç ʝ	x ɣ	χ ʁ	ħ ʕ	h ɦ
Lateral fricative				ɬ ɮ							
Approximant		ʋ		ɹ		ɻ	j	ɰ			
Lateral approximant				l		ɭ	ʎ	ʟ			

Where symbols appear in pairs, the one to the right represents a voiced consonant. Shaded areas denote articulations judged impossible.

CONSONANTS (NON-PULMONIC)

Clicks		Voiced implosives		Ejectives	
ʘ	Bilabial	ɓ	Bilabial	ʼ	Examples:
ǀ	Dental	ɗ	Dental/alveolar	pʼ	Bilabial
ǃ	(Post)alveolar	ʄ	Palatal	tʼ	Dental/alveolar
ǂ	Palatoalveolar	ɠ	Velar	kʼ	Velar
ǁ	Alveolar lateral	ʛ	Uvular	sʼ	Alveolar fricative

(Source: www.internationaphoneticalpahbet.org)

DIACRITICS Diacritics may be placed above a symbol with a descender, e.g. ŋ̊

◌̥	Voiceless	n̥ d̥	◌̤	Breathy voiced	b̤ a̤	◌̪	Dental	t̪ d̪
◌̬	Voiced	s̬ t̬	◌̰	Creaky voiced	b̰ a̰	◌̺	Apical	t̺ d̺
ʰ	Aspirated	tʰ dʰ	◌̼	Linguolabial	t̼ d̼	◌̻	Laminal	t̻ d̻
◌̹	More rounded	ɔ̹	ʷ	Labialized	tʷ dʷ	◌̃	Nasalized	ẽ
◌̜	Less rounded	ɔ̜	ʲ	Palatalized	tʲ dʲ	ⁿ	Nasal release	dⁿ
◌̟	Advanced	u̟	ˠ	Velarized	tˠ dˠ	ˡ	Lateral release	dˡ
◌̠	Retracted	e̠	ˤ	Pharyngealized	tˤ dˤ	◌̚	No audible release	d̚
◌̈	Centralized	ë	◌̴	Velarized or pharyngealized	ɫ			
◌̽	Mid-centralized	e̽	◌̝	Raised	e̝	(ɹ̝ = voiced alveolar fricative)		
◌̩	Syllabic	n̩	◌̞	Lowered	e̞	(β̞ = voiced bilabial approximant)		
◌̯	Non-syllabic	e̯	◌̘	Advanced Tongue Root	e̘			
˞	Rhoticity	ɚ a˞	◌̙	Retracted Tongue Root	e̙			

CONSONANTS (CO-ARTICULATED)

ʍ	Voiceless labialized velar approximant
w	Voiced labialized velar approximant
ɥ	Voiced labialized palatal approximant
ɕ	Voiceless palatalized postalveolar (alveolo-palatal) fricative
ʑ	Voiced palatalized postalveolar (alveolo-palatal) fricative
ɧ	Simultaneous *x* and *ʃ* (disputed)
k͡p t͜s	Affricates and double articulations may be joined by a tie bar

(Source: www.internationalphoneticalphabet.org)

References

1. Abibitumikasa.com. (Jan 5, 2010) Basic colors in Twi. Retrieved from https://www.abibitumikasa.com/forums/showthread.php/41686-Basic-colors-in-Twi
2. About.com. (n.d.) Adinkra Symbology. Retrieved from http://www. Africanhistory.about.com/library/weekly/aaAdrinkra.htm
3. Adolf H. Agbo, 1999, Values of Adinkra Symbols. Kumasi, Ghana: Ebony Designs and Publications.
4. International Phonetic Alphabet. (n.d.) IPA Chart with Sounds. Retrieved from http://www.internationalphoneticalphabet.org/ipa-chart-with-sounds/
5. Omniglot. (n.d.) Akan languages, alphabet and pronunciation. Retrieved from http://www.omniglot.com/writing/akan.htm
6. Omniglot (n.d.) Ewe (Evegbe). Retrieved from http://www.omniglot.com/writing/ewe.htm
7. Omniglot. (n.d.) Dagbani (Dagomba). Retrieved from http://www.omniglot.com/writing/dagbani.htm
8. Omniglot. (n.d.) Ga. Retrieved from http://www.omniglot.com/writing/ga.htm
9. G. F. Kojo Arthur, 2001, Cloth As Metaphor, (Re) Reading The Adinkra Cloth Symbols of The

Akan of Ghana. Accra, Ghana: Center for Indigenous Knowledge Systems(CEFIKS).

10. Ghanaculturepolitics.com (n.d.) The Ghana Anthem in Ewe. Retrieved from http://www.ghanaculturepolitics.com/the-ghana-anthem-in-ewe/
11. Ghanaculturepolitics.com (n.d.) The Ghana Anthem in Ga. Retrieved from http://ghanaculturepolitics.com/the-ghana-anthem-in-ga/
12. Ghana.gov. (n.d.) The National Anthem. Retrieved from http://www.ghana.gov.gh/index.php/about-ghana/the-national-anthem
13. West African Wisdom. (n.d.) Adinkra Symbols & Meanings. Retrieved from http://www.adinkra.org/htmls/adinkra_index._htm
14. W. Bruce Willis, 1998, The Adinkra Dictionary, A Visual Primer on The Language of Adinkra. Washington DC, USA: Pyramid Complex.
15. Wikipedia. (n.d.) Adinkra Symbols. Retrieved from https://en.wikipedia.org/wiki/Adinkra_Symbols
16. Wikipedia. (n.d.) Adinkra symbols (Physics). Retrieved from https://en.wikipedia.org/wiki/Adinkra_symbols_(physics)

17. Wikipedia. (n.d.) Akan Languages. Retrieved from https://en.wikipedia.org/wiki/Akan_language
18. Wikipedia. (n.d.) Astrological sign. Retrieved from https://en.wikipedia.org/wiki/Astrological_sign
19. Wikipedia. (n.d.) Ewe Language. Retrieved from http://en.wikipdeia.org/wiki/Ewe_language
20. Wikipedia. (n.d.) Dagbani Language. Retrieved from http://en.wikipedia.org/wiki/Dagbani_language
21. Wikipedia. (n.d.) Ga Language. Retrieved from http://en.wikipedia.org/wiki/Ga_language
22. Wikipedia. (n.d.) Phonetics. Retrieved from https://en.wikipedia.org/wiki/phonetics.
23. Wikipedia. (n.d.) Sefirot. Retrieved from https://en.wikipedia.org/wiki/sefirot

About the Author

I was born and raised in Ghana where I lived for the most part of my early and young adult life. I immigrated to the United States for completion of my Medical training in Family Medicine in 2006.
I have been practicing as a Family Medicine Physician Since 2011.

I have always had a great interest in symbols in general and the Adinkra Symbols in particular. The symbols were conceived and designed by craftsmen of Ancient African traditions.

This book uses these ancient and inspiring symbols to create an alphabet system and expand on their literal, physical and metaphysical significance in contemporary times.

Appendix I: Elemental property symbols

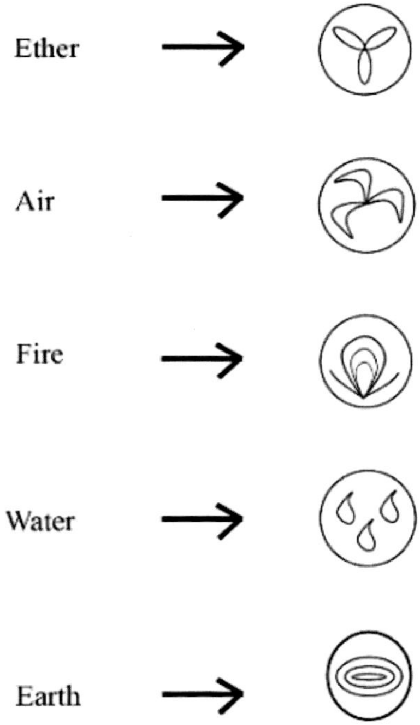
Ether
Air
Fire
Water
Earth

Appendix II: Adinkra Card Game

Adinkrahene
Mercy
3
a
Akofena
Courage
19,000
♂
Akokɔnan
Discipline
600
x
Akoma
Love
6,000
♍
Asase Ye Duru
Providence
200
r
Aya
Endurance
300
ι
Bese Saka
Resourcefulness
400
v
Bi Nka Bi
Peace
40
b
Boa Me Na Me
Mmoa Wo
Cooperation
16,000
☿

Appendix II – Cont.

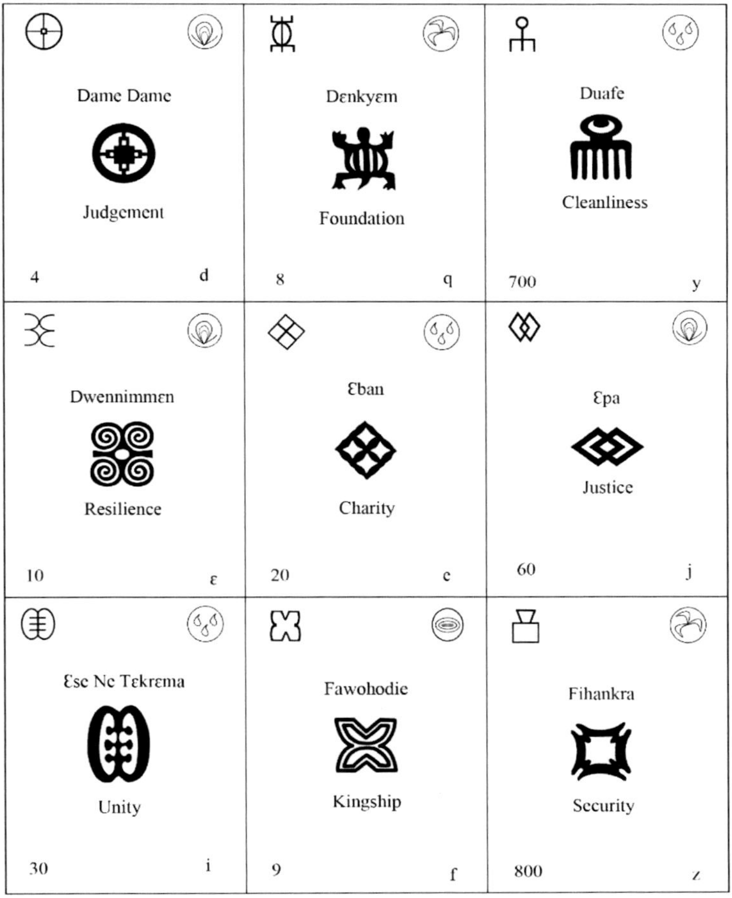
Dame Dame
Judgement
4
d
Dɛnkyɛm
Foundation
8
q
Duafe
Cleanliness
700
y
Dwennimmɛn
Resilience
10
ɛ
Ɛban
Charity
20
e
Ɛpa
Justice
60
j
Ɛse Ne Tɛkrɛma
Unity
30
i
Fawohodie
Kingship
9
f
Fihankra
Security
800
z

Appendix II – Cont.

Fofo  Transmutation 18,000 ⊕	Funtunfunefu Denkyɛmfunefu  Diversity 7,000 ♎	Gye Nyame  God 0 g
Hwemudua  Perfection 50 h	Hye Wonhye  Imperishability 1,000 ♈	Kɛtɛ Pa  Faith 13,000 ⛢
Kintinkantan  Humility 70 k	Kwatakye Atikɔ  Bravery 20,000 ♃	Mate Masie  Prudence 11,000 ♒

Appendix II – Cont.

Mframadan  Fortitude — 10,000 ♑	Mmerɛ Dane  Constancy — 80 l	Mpatapɔ  Reconciliation — 90 m
Mpuanum  Skillfulness — 5,000 ♌	Musuyidɛɛ  Enlightenment — 21,000 ♄	Nea Onnim No Sua A, Ohu  Service — 7 u
Nkɔnsɔnkɔnsɔn  Responsibility — 8,000 ♏	Nkyimu 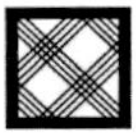 Precision — 100 n	Nkyinkyim  Adaptability — 12,000 ♓

Appendix II – Cont.

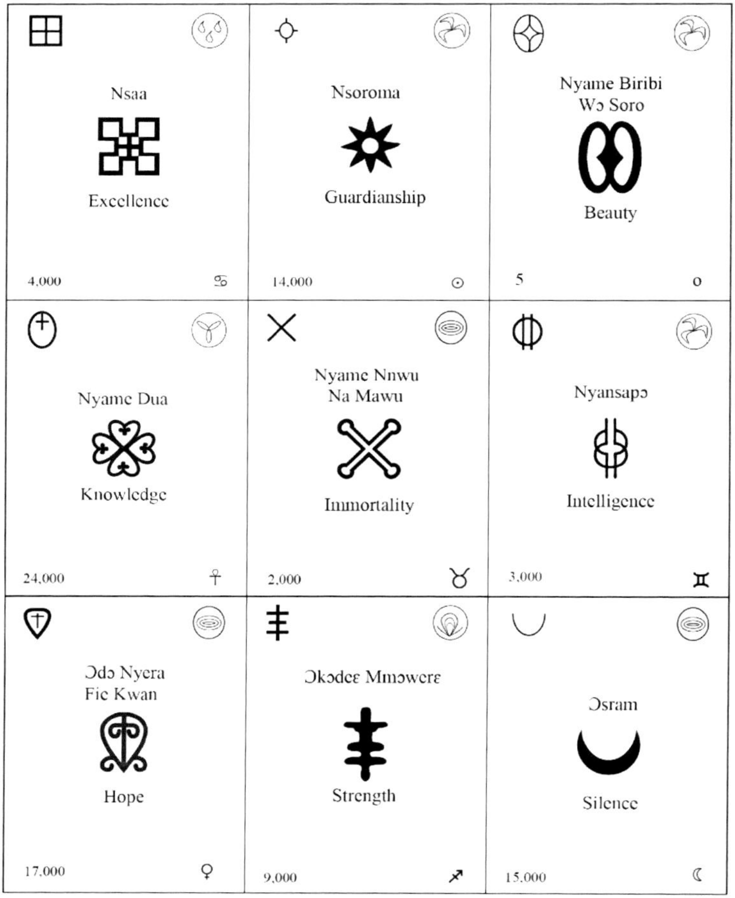
Nsaa
Excellence
4,000
Nsoroma
Guardianship
14,000
Nyame Biribi Wɔ Soro
Beauty
5
o
Nyame Dua
Knowledge
24,000
Nyame Nnwu Na Mawu
Immortality
2,000
Nyansapɔ
Intelligence
3,000
Ɔdɔ Nyera Fie Kwan
Hope
17,000
Ɔkɔdeɛ Mmɔwerɛ
Strength
9,000
Ɔsram
Silence
15,000

Appendix II – Cont.

Ɔsram Ne Nsoromma  Harmony 900 ɔ	Ɔwɔ Foro Adobɛ 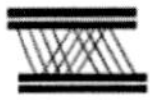 Victory 6 c	Owuo Atwedeɛ  Mortality 22,000 ♅
Pempamsie  Understanding 2 p	Sankɔfa  Wisdom 1 s	Sunsum  Soul 23,000 ♆
Wawa Aba  Perseverance 500 w		

Appendix III: Adinkra and Sypersymmetry

In supergravity theory, sypersymmetry theory and superstring theory, 'Adinkra symbols' are a graphical representation of supersymmetric algebras. The similarity between 'Adinkra' in supersymmetry and Adinkra symbols in general is that they are both graphical representations with hidden meanings. The supersymmetry graph shows colored dots connected with simple lines as shown below. In string, superstring and supersymmetry theory the 11 dimensions of space is related to the 11 spheres of the Adinkra Tree of Life (ATOL).

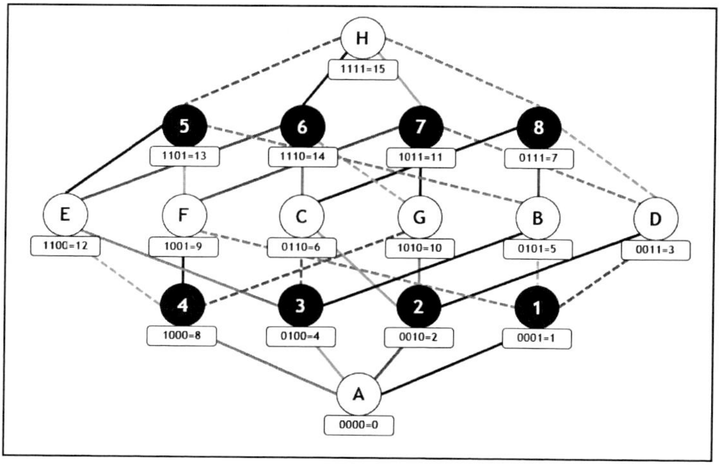
H
1111=15
5
1101=13
6
1110=14
7
1011=11
8
0111=7
E
1100=12
F
1001=9
C
0110=6
G
1010=10
B
0101=5
D
0011=3
4
1000=8
3
0100=4
2
0010=2
1
0001=1
A
0000=0

S. James Gates, Jr. explains how research on a class of geometric symbols known as adinkras could lead to fresh insights into the theory of supersymmetry — and perhaps even the very nature of reality.

Appendix IV: Adinkra Alphabet

ADINKRA ALPHABET

Akan, Ewe, Ga and Dagbani

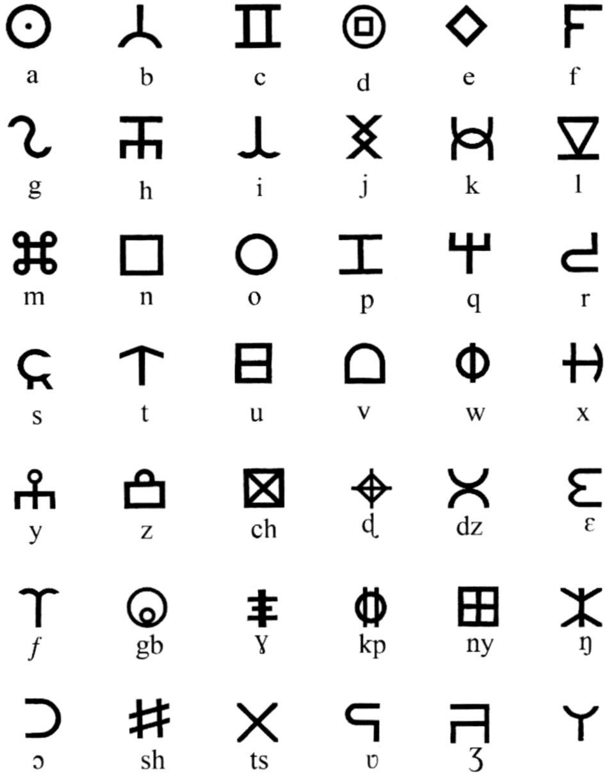
a b c d e f
g h i j k l
m n o p q r
s t u v w x
y z ch ɖ dz ɛ
ƒ gb ɣ kp ny ŋ
ɔ sh ts ʋ ʒ

Appendix IV: Adinkra Alphabet – Cont.

ADINKRA ALPHABET

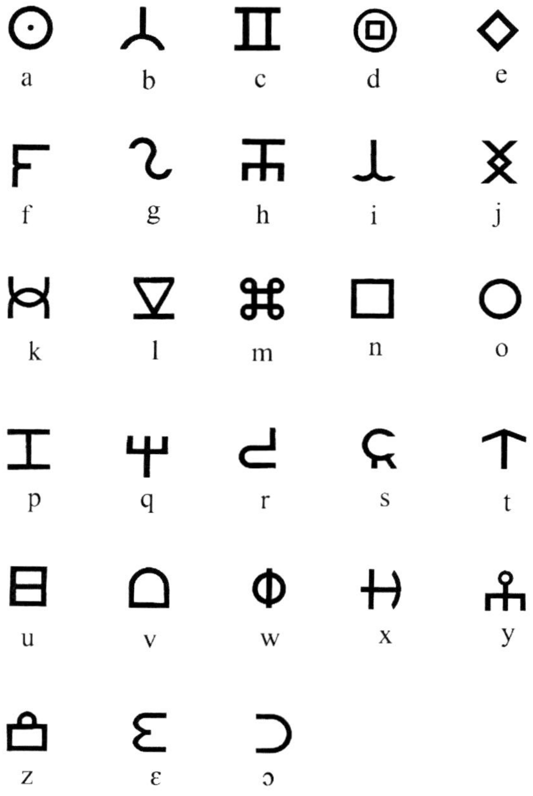
a
b
c
d
e
f
g
h
i
j
k
l
m
n
o
p
q
r
s
t
u
v
w
x
y
z
ɛ
ɔ

Appendix IV: Adinkra Alphabet – Cont.

ADINKRA ALPHABET

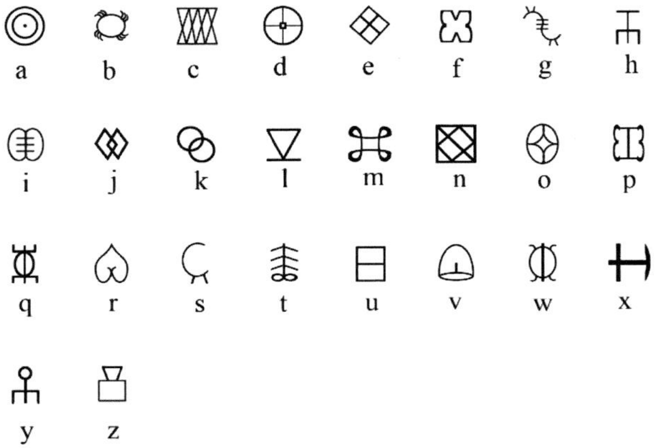
a b c d e f g h
i j k l m n o p
q r s t u v w x
y z

SPECIAL CHARACTERS FOR AKAN, EWE, GA AND DAGBANI

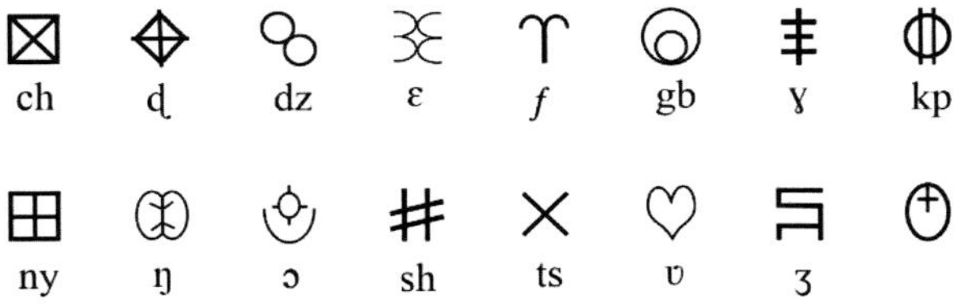
ch ɖ dz ɛ ƒ gb ɣ kp
ny ŋ ɔ sh ts ʋ ʒ

Appendix IV: Adinkra Alphabet – Cont.

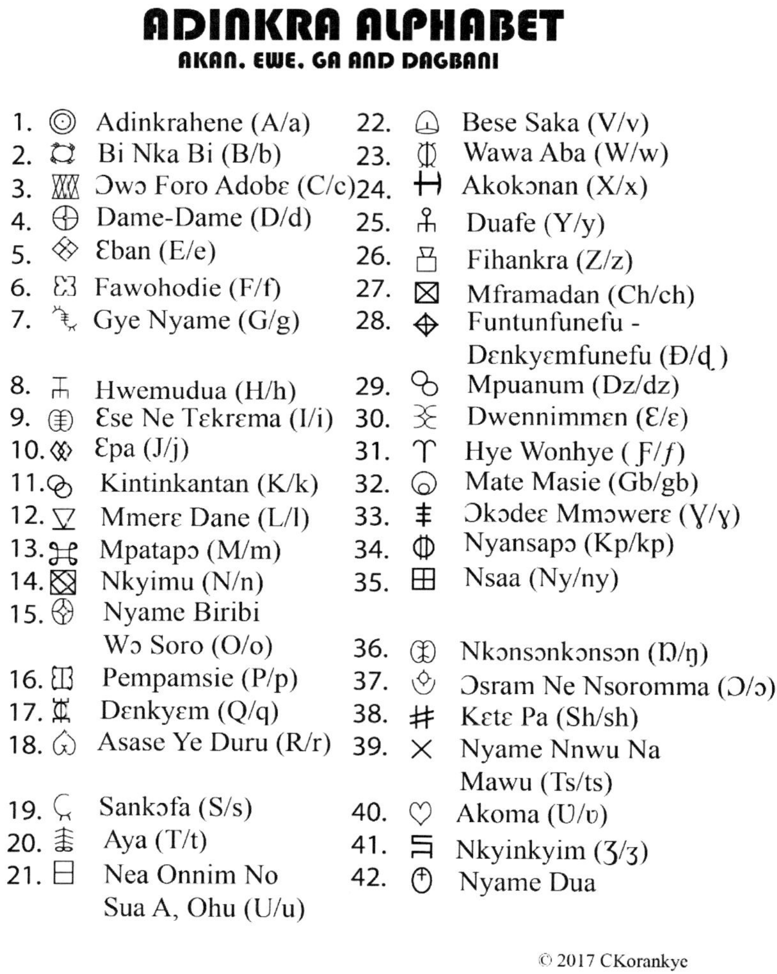

ADINKRA ALPHABET
AKAN, EWE, GA AND DAGBANI

1. Adinkrahene (A/a)
2. Bi Nka Bi (B/b)
3. Ɔwɔ Foro Adobɛ (C/c)
4. Dame-Dame (D/d)
5. Ɛban (E/e)
6. Fawohodie (F/f)
7. Gye Nyame (G/g)
8. Hwemudua (H/h)
9. Ɛse Ne Tɛkrɛma (I/i)
10. Ɛpa (J/j)
11. Kintinkantan (K/k)
12. Mmerɛ Dane (L/l)
13. Mpatapɔ (M/m)
14. Nkyimu (N/n)
15. Nyame Biribi Wɔ Soro (O/o)
16. Pempamsie (P/p)
17. Dɛnkyɛm (Q/q)
18. Asase Ye Duru (R/r)
19. Sankɔfa (S/s)
20. Aya (T/t)
21. Nea Onnim No Sua A, Ohu (U/u)
22. Bese Saka (V/v)
23. Wawa Aba (W/w)
24. Akokɔnan (X/x)
25. Duafe (Y/y)
26. Fihankra (Z/z)
27. Mframadan (Ch/ch)
28. Funtunfunefu - Dɛnkyɛmfunefu (Đ/ɖ)
29. Mpuanum (Dz/dz)
30. Dwennimmɛn (Ɛ/ɛ)
31. Hye Wonhye (Ƒ/ƒ)
32. Mate Masie (Gb/gb)
33. Ɔkɔdeɛ Mmɔwerɛ (Ɣ/ɣ)
34. Nyansapɔ (Kp/kp)
35. Nsaa (Ny/ny)
36. Nkɔnsɔnkɔnsɔn (Ŋ/ŋ)
37. Ɔsram Ne Nsoromma (Ɔ/ɔ)
38. Kɛtɛ Pa (Sh/sh)
39. Nyame Nnwu Na Mawu (Ts/ts)
40. Akoma (Ʊ/ʊ)
41. Nkyinkyim (Ʒ/ʒ)
42. Nyame Dua

Appendix IV: Adinkra Alphabet – Cont.

ADINKRA ALPHABET

AKAN, EWE, GA AND DAGBANI

1. Adinkrahene (A/a)
2. Bi Nka Bi (B/b)
3. Ɔwɔ Foro Adobɛ (C/c)
4. Dame-Dame (D/d)
5. Ɛban (E/e)
6. Fawohodie (F/f)
7. Gye Nyame (G/g)
8. Hwemudua (H/h)
9. Ɛse Ne Tɛkrɛma (I/i)
10. Ɛpa (J/j)
11. Kintinkantan (K/k)
12. Mmerɛ Dane (L/l)
13. Mpatapɔ (M/m)
14. Nkyimu (N/n)
15. Nyame Biribi Wɔ Soro (O/o)
16. Pempamsie (P/p)
17. Dɛnkyɛm (Q/q)
18. Asase Ye Duru (R/r)
19. Sankɔfa (S/s)
20. Aya (T/t)
21. Nea Onnim No Sua A Ohu (U/u)
22. Bese Saka (V/v)
23. Wawa Aba (W/w)
24. Akokɔnan (X/x)
25. Duafe (Y/y)
26. Fihankra (Z/z)
27. Mframadan (Ch/ch)
28. Funtunfunefu-Dɛnkyɛmfunefu (Ɖ/ɖ)
29. Mpuanum (Dz/dz)
30. Dwennimmɛn (Ɛ/ɛ)
31. Hye Wonhye (Ƒ/ƒ)
32. Mate Masie (Gb/gb)
33. Ɔkɔdeɛ Mmɔwerɛ (Ɣ/ɣ)
34. Nyansapɔ (Kp/kp)
35. Nsaa (Ny/ny)
36. Nkɔnsɔnkɔnsɔn (Ŋ/ŋ)
37. Ɔsram Ne Nsoromma (Ɔ/ɔ)
38. Kɛtɛ Pa (Sh/sh)
39. Nyame Nnwu Na Mawu (Ts/ts)
40. Akoma (Ʊ/ʊ)
41. Nkyinkyim (Ʒ/ʒ)
42. Nyame Dua

Index

A

Adinkra, ii, iii, i, 2, 3, 4, 5, 6, 8, 12, 13, 14, 15, 16, 17, 18, 19, 20, 21, 22, 23, 24, 25, 26, 27, 90, 91, 93, 105, 106, 109, 123, 155, 158, 159, 185, 188, 189, 190, 191, 192, 194, 195, 196, 198, 199, 200, 202, 203, 204, 206, 207, 208, 212, 215, 216, 218, 219, 221, 223, 224, 226, 227, 228, 229, 231, 234, 235, 236, 237, 238, 239, 241, 242, 243, 244, 245, 246, 247, 250, 251, 252, 255, 256, 258
Adinkra Alphabet, iii, iv, viii, ix, x, xiii, 5, 6, 27, 28, 29, 30, 31, 32, 33, 34, 35, 36, 37, 38, 39, 40, 41, 42, 43, 44, 45, 46, 47, 48, 49, 50, 51, 52, 53, 54, 55, 56, 57, 58, 59, 60, 61, 62, 63, 64, 65, 66, 67, 68, 69, 70, 71, 72, 73, 74, 75, 76, 77, 78, 79, 80, 92, 112, 123, 210, 212, 215, 216, 226, 227, 228, 234, 235, 236, 242, 243, 244, 250, 251, 252, 260, 267, 268, 269, 270
Adinkra and Sypersymmetry, 266
Adinkra Astronomical Sign, 121, 122
Adinkra Astronomy, 120
Adinkra card game, x
Adinkra Flower of Life, x, 92, 97, 118
Adinkra symbols, ix, x, i, 3, 6, 26, 90, 177, 256, 266
Adinkra Tree of Life, iv, x, 90, 92, 97, 118, 266
Adinkra Zodiac, 119
Adinkrahene, 7, 12, 27, 91, 93, 105, 159, 189
AFOL, x, 77, 97, 98, 116, 118
African countries, 123
African Countries, 147
Airway, 217
Airway Position of Consonants, 217
Akan language, 4
Akan Proverb, 177, 178, 179, 180, 181, 182, 183, 184
Akoben, 73, 74, 108, 183
Akofena, 74, 108, 114, 174, 184
Akokonan, 8, 20, 21, 22, 23, 24, 25, 50, 106, 166

Akoma, 62, 107, 114, 170, 181
alphabet, i, 2, 5, 6, 8, 26, 123, 185, 255, 258
Alveolar, 186, 215, 227, 235, 243, 251
Approximants, 187
Asantehene, 3
Asase Ye Duru, 8, 18, 45, 164
ATOL, x, 77, 90, 92, 109, 116, 118, 266
Aya, 8, 19, 47, 106, 165

B

beauty, 51, 188
Bese Saka, 8, 19, 48, 106, 166
Bi Nka Bi, 4, 14, 32, 159
bilabial, 186
Boa Me Na Me Mmoa Wo, 70, 108, 173, 183

Ɔ

Ɔdɔ Nyera Fie Kwan, 71, 114, 173, 183
Ɔkɔdeɛ Mmɔwerɛ, 59, 107, 113, 171, 182

C

Consonant, 191, 192, 195, 196, 199, 200, 203, 204, 207, 208, 221, 222, 223, 224, 231, 232, 233, 239, 240, 241, 247, 248, 249
Consonants, 8, 14, 32, 185, 191, 215, 221, 227, 231, 235, 239, 243, 247, 251, 253
creation, xiii, 6, 90, 91, 186
Creator, 79, 90, 91
crown, 188

Ɔ

Ɔsram, 6, 13, 54, 69, 107, 108, 109, 114, 168, 173, 180, 183

D

Dame-Dame, 14, 34, 91, 93, 160, 189
Dark Energy-Dark Matter, 91, 98
Denkyɛm, 8, 18, 44, 92, 93, 105, 164, 189
dental, 186, 215, 227, 235, 243, 251
Duafe, 8, 20, 21, 22, 23, 24, 25, 51, 106, 167
Dwennimmen, 6, 53, 105, 109, 167

E

Eban, 7, 12, 28, 105, 160
Epa, 4, 8, 16, 38, 106, 162
Ese Ne Tekrema, 7, 12, 161
Extended Adinkra alphabet, 6

F

Fawohodie, 15, 35, 90, 92, 93, 160, 189
Fihankra, 8, 20, 21, 22, 23, 24, 25, 52, 106, 167
Fofo, 72, 108, 114, 174, 183
foundation, 90, 188
Fricative, 186, 189, 215, 216, 227, 228, 235, 236, 243, 244, 251, 252
Funtunfunefu Dɛnkyɛmfunefu, 55

G

Geometrical, 110
Ghana, xiii, i, 4, 5, 6, 34, 123, 124, 130, 255, 258
Ghana National Anthem, 123, 124, 130
Ghana National Anthem Akan, 136
Ghana National Anthem Dagbani, 145
Ghana National Anthem English, 139
Ghana National Anthem Ewe, 141
Ghana National Anthem Ga, 143
glottal, 186
God, 13, 15, 24, 25, 30, 36, 63, 79, 80, 90, 91, 140, 178, 179, 181, 184
Greater Light, 91

Gyawu Atikɔ, 75, 76, 108, 175, 184
Gye Nyame, 4, 15, 36, 91, 93, 161, 189

H

Hidden Meanings, iii
Hwemudua, 15, 37, 161
Hye Wonhye, 57, 107, 109, 113, 168, 181

I

International Phonetic Alphabet system, 185
Ivory Coast, 3

J

judgment, 34, 91

K

Kabbalah, 90
Kɛtɛ Pa, 66, 98, 108, 112, 172, 183
Kingdom, 93, 188, 189
Kintinkantan, 16, 39, 106, 162
Knowledge, 92, 256
Kwatakye Atikɔ, 75, 76, 108, 114, 175, 184

L

labiodental, 186
Lateral approximant, 187, 215, 216, 227, 228, 235, 236, 243, 244, 251, 252
Lateral fricatives, 187
Literal meaning, 5, 27, 28, 29, 30, 31, 32, 33, 34, 35, 36, 37, 38, 39, 40, 41, 42, 43, 44, 45, 46, 47, 48, 49, 50, 51, 52, 53, 54

M

Mate Masie, 58, 107, 113, 171, 182

Mercy, 91, 93, 189
metaphysical, 2, 5, 26, 90, 91, 258
Metaphysical meaning, 2, 5, 26, 27, 28, 29, 30, 31, 32, 33, 34, 35, 36, 37, 38, 39, 40, 41, 42, 43, 44, 45, 46, 47, 48, 49, 50, 51, 52, 53, 54, 110, 111
Mframadan, 65, 107, 114, 171, 182
middle pathway, 90, 188
Mmere Dane, 8, 16, 40, 106, 162
Mpatapo, 4, 17, 41, 106, 163
Mpuanum, 56, 107, 113, 169, 181
Musuyideɛ, 77, 113, 175, 184

N

nasal, 186, 188
Nea Onnim No Sua A, Ohu, 31
Nkɔnsɔnkɔnsɔn, 23, 64, 107, 114, 170, 182
Nkyimu, 17, 42, 106, 163
Nkyinkyim, 67, 107, 114, 172, 182
Nsaa, 61, 107, 114, 169, 181
Nsoromma, 4, 13, 54, 68, 107, 108, 109, 113, 114, 168, 172, 180, 183
Numbering System, 155
Numerical value, 27, 28, 29, 30, 31, 32, 33, 34, 35, 36, 37, 38, 39, 40, 41, 42, 43, 44, 45, 46, 47, 48, 49, 50, 51, 52, 53, 54, 105
Numerology, 105, 109, 110
Nyame Biribi Wo Soro, 7, 13, 30, 92, 93, 163
Nyame Dua, 7, 13, 80, 92, 93, 97, 98, 105, 108, 109, 112, 165, 176, 184, 189
Nyame Nwu Na Mawu, 63, 181
Nyansapɔ, 60, 107, 113, 169, 181

O

Osram Ne Nsoromma, 6, 54, 106, 168
Owo Foro Adobe, 8, 14, 33, 92, 93, 159, 189
Owuo Atwedeɛ, 78, 108, 114, 176, 184

P

palatal, 186, 225
palate, 185, 186
Pempamsie, 17, 43, 91, 93, 105, 164, 189
pharyngeal, 186
Phonetics, 185, 257
physical meaning, 2, 26
Physical meaning, 5, 27, 28, 29, 30, 31, 32, 33, 34, 35, 36, 37, 38, 39, 40, 41, 42, 43, 44, 45, 46, 47, 48, 49, 50, 51, 52, 53, 54, 110, 111
Plosive, 188, 189, 215, 216, 227, 228, 235, 236, 243, 244, 251, 252
Primary Adinkra alphabet, 6
Pronunciation, 218, 219, 221, 222, 223, 224, 229, 231, 232, 233, 237, 238, 239, 240, 241, 245, 246, 247, 248, 249
Proverbs, 177

R

Retroflex, 186, 215, 227, 235, 243, 251

S

Sankofa, 18, 46, 91, 93, 105, 165, 189
Sephirot, 90, 91
Sunsum, 79, 98, 108, 109, 112, 176, 184
symbol, 2, 4, 6, 7, 8, 26, 27, 32, 38, 54, 90

T

teeth, 29, 185, 186
The Creator, 90
The Greater Light, 91, 98
Thrill, 188, 189
throat, 185, 186
tongue, 29, 185, 186, 187, 188
Tongue Position of Vowels, 213
Tree of Life, 26, 90, 91, 109, 186, 188, 189

U

understanding, i, 90, 91
Understanding, x, 69, 97

V

velar, 186
Victory, 92, 93, 189
vortices of energy, 90, 91
Vowels, 7, 12, 27, 185, 190, 212, 214, 218, 226, 229, 234, 237, 242, 245, 250

W

Wawa Aba, 19, 49, 106, 166
West Africa, i
Wisdom, 46, 91, 93, 189, 256

Y

Yen Ara Asase Ni, 137

Adinkra Alphabet